Can You Run Your Business With Blood, Sweat, and Tears? Volume III

Can You Run Your Business With Blood, Sweat, and Tears? Volume III

Tears

Stephen Elkins-Jarrett
Nick Skinner

 BUSINESS EXPERT PRESS

First published in 2018 by
Business Expert Press, LLC
222 East 46th Street, New York, NY 10017
www.businessexpertpress.com

ISBN-13: 978-1-94858-040-3 (paperback)
ISBN-13: 978-1-94858-041-0 (e-book)

Business Expert Press Entrepreneurship and Small Business Management Collection

Collection ISSN: 1946-5653 (print)
Collection ISSN: 1946-5661 (electronic)

Cover and interior design by S4Carlisle Publishing Services Private Ltd., Chennai, India

First edition: 2018

10 9 8 7 6 5 4 3 2 1

Printed in the United States of America.

Dedication

For Eddie and Leia

TRAINING
ENCOURAGEMENT
ANNOUNCEMENT
REVIEW
SUCCESS

Abstract

What does it take to successfully lead and manage a business or a team? Management consultant and HR specialist Stephen-Elkins Jarrett and organizational development consultant Nick Skinner share their combined experience of how mastery of 15 key areas can help you drive your business, team, or even yourself to success. Presented using the acronym of BLOOD, SWEAT, and TEARS, this book, presented in three volumes, aligns some established models with common sense to give a practical view with tools and tips gained over years of working across different industries and sectors. At the heart of the book is the fascinating study of behavior, discussed through the SPECTRUM model of behavior, showing how by treating others in the way that they want to be treated, we can engage, develop, and lead them to achieve meaningful goals.

Keywords

behavior, development, HR, human resources, leadership, management, performance, SPECTRUM, strategy, team, teamwork

Contents

Foreword

Blood, Sweat, and Tears

Elkins-Jarrett & Skinner

Stephen and Nick have packed a huge amount into the volumes of this trilogy. Their years of business consulting experience is evident as they make every element wholly understandable and immensely practical—this is not a book about business theory; it is a book to be put into immediate action.

Using the acronym B-L-O-O-D S-W-E-A-T-and-T-E-A-R-S, they consider 16 areas of importance in business success (the "and" is an important area, hence 16) and within these incorporate aspects as disparate as time management, presentation skills, work–life balance, vision, and performance management, in addition to the chapter titles such as Brand, Leadership, Opportunities, and so forth using illustrations from areas as diverse as Psychology and Star Wars.

Running through the book is the recurring theme of understanding and appreciating human behavior in its many facets. They expound "Spectrum" behavioral psychometric, which fits with the themes of their book—approachable, easy to understand, and practical. All other Jungian models would also work, but I agree with them that Spectrum's simplicity enhances the ability to apply the learning effortlessly and across all cultures.

Throughout the chapters, they make use of well-known, tried-and-tested theories including Tuckman, Maslow, Kotter, and Hersey & Blanchard—only models and structures that have stood the test of time rather than any that are likely to be in vogue today and forgotten tomorrow. Within these, they give their own adaptations and developments driven by decades of management consulting experience, which make them more practical and more applicable.

If you are looking for a book that covers a wide range of criteria for business success and is eminently readable, down-to-earth, practical, and developed through the crucible of decades of experience, Blood, Sweat, and Tears is a wise choice.

Stephen Berry

MBA, MSc, BSc(Hons), FCMA, CGMA, ACIB, DipFS, PgD
Author of *Strategies of the Serengeti* (2006; 2nd ed., 2010)
and
Teach Yourself Strategy in a Week (2012; 2nd ed., 2016)

Introduction to Blood, Sweat, and Tears

"I have nothing to offer except blood, sweat and tears!" paraphrased from a speech given to the UK houses of parliament in the dark days of 1940 by Prime Minister Sir Winston Churchill.

Hello and welcome to "Blood, Sweat, and Tears!" Why did we write it? What is it all about? And who the heck are these guys anyway?

Stephen's Story

My story is that I have been working since I was 16. My background is strange but has given me an insight into the commercial world that others don't get. I did not have a classical educational background. My parents divorced when I was 11. My father was in sales and my mother a sports teacher and legal secretary. At 16, my mother said "leave school and go to work, we need the money." I trained as a chef, day release at Slough College, near Heathrow airport, and I left after I had completed my OND and HND (Ordinary and Higher National Diplomas) to work with my father in the construction industry. I qualified in NFBPM at Diploma level. At the same time, I was involved in Amateur Dramatics. While in a play, I was approached by a director who asked me if I fancied quitting my job to be his personal assistant and learn his trade from the bottom. He was a Coopers and Lybrand Management Consultant, now running his own business. This was a single act of kindness that changed my world forever.

I went to night school to do my A levels, did a distance learning Degree with UEL in Industrial Psychology—now called Organizational. I then qualified in Psychometrics, Life Coaching, NLP, CBT, did an advanced Diploma in Organizational Psychology at Oxford learning and then finally got my Master's in Organizational Psychology just a few years ago. Parallel to this, I worked full time for Mike at Manskill

Associates, watching, learning, listening, and delivering soft skill training, facilitated workshops, strategy workshops, leadership development, and management and supervisory training and coaching. I also joined the CIPD and learned everything I could about HR and worked in HR departments as an interim for some great HR directors such as Julie Sutton and talent directors such as Joanne Rye. I worked as an interim HR director, HR manager, employee relations manager, caseworker, a TUPE project manager, change, takeovers, mergers, and acquisitions. I saw and learned more from this strange and unusual journey through the commercial world than I would have done with a "proper Job" as my wife calls it and in a traditional career along the way. I worked in catering, hospitality, healthcare, and pharmaceutical industries, and in scientific institutions and laboratories. I had also worked in construction, property, IT, finance, banking, FMCG, utilities, high-voltage power stations, supermarkets, motor industry, and several others, delivering soft skills training, group facilitation, coaching, team work and team building, and lots more. In totality, I have worked in the biggest and the smallest and everything in between; and one thing remained constant for me—it is all the same. When recruiters look for someone with managerial experience in a certain industry, any manager could learn the new job, but man management skills remain a constant. Eighty percent is behavior and twenty percent technical skills and knowledge; and you can learn this bit as you go. Richard Branson said, "If anyone asks you if you can do this job, say yes and then learn it as you go." He has always done this.

Nick's Story

My story is almost the opposite. Raised in Hertfordshire, I scrapped the grades needed to do a first degree before taking up a graduate job, providing business and project accounting support to scientists. This was in the late 1980s and the UK was still reeling from the impacts of Thatcherism, where large swathes of the UK infrastructure that had traditionally been operated using public money were being forced down a route that made them think more commercially. The reaction to the kind of externally and politically induced change created an organizational stress that taught me a lot. I realized quickly that while finance was important, there was more to business than the accountant's view. Hence, I shifted away from finance and into broader business commercial management, completing an MBA with distinction in 1997 from the University of Hertfordshire and then shifting my career to London to work in the field of commercializing intellectual property, working as a business administrator for a spin-out company commercializing breakthroughs in cancer technology, developing plans for seed funds and managing a large network of technology transfer stakeholders. Again, in this role, I was providing commercial and business support to some very clever scientists. I moved back into agricultural sciences in 1999, working on business plans and change programs in that sphere for the next 13 years. It was a long time, but there were so many projects and exciting new businesses being developed that it was really more like four or five different jobs. Certainly, by the time I moved on from there, I had earned my projects management wings, acting as the leader of a number of change programs which (mostly) went according to plan. There were some car crashes of course, but they got fewer, so I must have been getting better! Sometime while there, I attended an eye-opening training program and came across some very bright cookies doing organizational development at Roffey Park. My training with these guys made me finally realize that what really goes on in business is human interaction, and that to get great outcomes in business all you needed was great humans. Then it all started to fall in place. Great business outcomes are about great people, so if all humans are great this should be easy, right? Wrong! There's so much that we humans create and fantasize about and are scared of that prevent us from being at our best. I strongly believe that organizations that can remove these blocks and find a proper level of human connection can build trust and once you have trust then we can really start to go places. I took an MSc in organizational and people development through Roffey Park and in 2012 backed my learning with the establishment of Poppyfish People Development, thereby fulfilling a career dream of helping business capitalize on the potential of the human in the system and engaging in client work across multiple industries and coming across Steve Jarrett, and his SPECTRUM model in 2013. As opposites attract, we make a good team.

Coming Together

We met when a mutual friend and client, Ian Cresswell, a people-focused leader to whom we are both indebted, intuitively thought we would work well together in his organization. We did. Nick is more cautious and careful, methodical, analytical, and checks everything and Stephen, dives in, cracks on, and says, "Everything will be alright in the end, if it is not alright it is not the end!" (Indian Proverb). Stephen thinks getting stuck in is the answer and Nick knows that to reflect and think about it first often gets a better outcome. Nick acts as the brake to Stephen's accelerator pedal and on average we work off each other well. Like in many relationships, the only challenges come when we both want to steer. We both believe in the power of dreams and that positivity and energy really count for something.

Our work together has been varied, and challenging, but always rewarding, working as coaches, consultants, trainers, facilitators, and leaders of learning and behavior change for many individuals, teams, and businesses. In a nutshell, we help our clients align people performance with organization performance. We do this in many different industry sectors, including technical services, information technology, scientific research, start-ups, and construction. We don't spend much on marketing; instead, our growth has been through word of mouth and personal recommendation. We think that is important. It's part of our own brand.

We are guided by the simple principle that the best people build the best businesses. In a world increasingly driven by technical development and big data, workplaces remain a human environment. The performance of your business depends massively upon the talents, motivations, and behaviors of the people who work within it.

We want to see those people at their best, in a space where their talents shine.

To work with us is to recognize that each of us has our own dreams, aspirations, and desires, and that if we can tap into this rich vein of motivation, then we can all fly. Our motives for writing this series of books are to capture some of the "common sense" activities that we think make a difference to how businesses perform. Most of what you will read here is not rocket science, but it is hopefully practical and resonates enough with your own experiences to allow you to feel confident and capable at making great things happen. It's a chance for us to share what we have learnt through the blood, sweat, and tears of our work, and we hope that you find the content rewarding.

Blood, Sweat, and Tears

"Blood, Sweat, and Tears" is a simple-to-follow trilogy of books offering most of the advice you would need to develop, grow, and succeed as a manager or leader in any team or business from a one-man self-employed person to a large enterprise. The ideas in this set of books have come about after many years of consulting practice—working with the great, the good (and even the bad). From seeing businesses fail and learning from their mistakes through to business that did great things and were successful, the authors have picked up the best practices and principles that guide one to success. These books attempt to share our learning. The principles, ideas, and ways of thinking that are outlined in these pages will help to focus your thinking with regard to self-development, team development, and business development.

According to Bloomberg, 8 out of 10 entrepreneurs who start businesses fail within the first 18 months. A whopping 80 percent crash and burn after having the chance to send out only one lot of corporate Christmas cards. But why? The reasons that businesses fail are painful in that as much as many of these failures are easily avoidable.

At surface level, the primary reason businesses fail is that they run out of cash. But the reasons for that are deeper than apparent shallowness of the cash drawer. In our combined lives as consultants, we have seen plenty, advised many, and been ignored by lots!

How can you avoid these failures? Only through the application of "blood, sweat, and tears."

We have created BLOOD, SWEAT, and TEARS as acronyms for all the things that you can do that will help to drive success; setting out attitudes, behaviors, and practices that you can follow to help you achieve your and your company's goals. The ideas are developed throughout the following pages, with each letter of the acronyms given its own chapter. The acronyms are summarized here in brief:

Book One

BLOOD is the life source of your success.

> **B** stands for **BRAND**: Can you build the right brand for you and for your business and demonstrate alignment between the two?
>
> **L** stands for **LEADERSHIP**: Do you have the right skills to understand the needs of others and get the best out of yourself and your team?
>
> **O** stands for **OPPORTUNITIES**: Can you manage the process of generating leads and prospects and take advantage of the opportunities that will grow your business?
>
> **O** stands for **OUTCOMES**: Are you focusing on the right outcomes to hit your goals? How do you set goals and objectives?
>
> **D** is for **DECISIONS**: Can you make the right decisions that lead to success?

Book Two

SWEAT is symbolic of the exercises that you should constantly be focused on.

> **S** stands for **STRATEGIC DIRECTION**: Do you have the right vision, mission, strategy, and structure for your business to succeed?
>
> **W** stands for **WHAT IF?**: Do you know what to do in those "What If . . ." moments? Can you and your team be resilient or forward thinking enough to take steps to avoid confusion and chaos in a fast-changing world?
>
> **E** stands for **EVIDENCE**: Can you find the evidence to back your intuition? What can you do to get the information you need to act for the best?
>
> **A** stands for **ACTION**: Can you overcome the urge to procrastinate and take action when you need to?
>
> **T** stands for **TIME**: Can you get your timings right and manage everything you have to do in a way that keeps you in control?

Don't forget the **and** (**&**): Don't forget yourself and enjoyment and quality time and family and friends, etc.

Book Three

TEARS are the things that will refresh and reward you.

> **T** stands for **TRAINING**: Are you training the right people in the right way? The essential tool that makes you ready to cope with the demands of tomorrow. Train people all the time and so they can leave—then treat them so they don't want to!
>
> **E** is for **ENCOURAGEMENT**: To get the best out of others, you must know what drives and motivates them. Can you give encouragement to others and know where to find your own?
>
> **A** stands for **ANNOUNCEMENTS**: Do you announce the important things in the right way? How can you present for maximum impact?
>
> **R** stands for **REVIEW**: Do you take time to reflect and review the past with an eye on the future? Taking time at each step of the way to look back at what you have achieved, what you can learn from it, and how this can help you for future planning.
>
> **S** stands for **SUCCESS**: Can you deliver success for you, your team, and your business? How will you know you are succeeding and what to do next? Taking time to enjoy your successes has a narcotic effect, leaving you wanting more!

Our experience tells us that this is what makes a difference in successful organizations. If you get it right, the benefits can be stunning. Here's what happens if you get it wrong:

If you cannot identify or build your **BRAND,** then you'll be faced with confused customers and staff who don't really know what the business (or you, if you are the brand) stands for. You'll have to accept that others will define it for you.

If you do not develop the right **LEADERSHIP** skills, you will create anxiety and frustration for others and increase the propensity for false starts and you will have to accept that people will be frustrated. You will start to lose people, starting with the best ones first.

If you fail to act on **OPPORTUNITIES,** then you can expect finances to take a direct hit. The implications of this are obvious. While this is playing out, you will generate anxiety for people who will realize that the writing is on the wall.

If you fail to identify the right **OUTCOMES,** then people do the wrong thing. False starts happen and people get frustrated and confused. You cannot track progress. Tasks never finish. Morale drops. People leave. And so do customers.

If you struggle with **DECISIONS,** then you can expect people to get frustrated and for confusion to reign. Lack of decision making provokes anxiety and slows your business down.

If you fail to define and communicate a **STRATEGIC DIRECTION,** then chaos abounds. Your business becomes a lawless territory without guidance or a moral compass. People make up their own strategy and resist your efforts to pull them away from that because they do not know any better. You will never have buy in and without buy in you will be in a state of constant confusion. You will also be handing over control to the micro-managers.

If you fail to spot and train yourselves for the **WHAT IF . . .** moments, then you will create anxiety as people will not feel equipped to deal with change and you will be left behind by the world. You also risk jeopardizing your business by reducing its resilience to the point where the slightest wave or market tremor could threaten its existence.

If you fail to secure **EVIDENCE** for changes, you will cause frustration and run the risk of a number of false starts where you thought you were doing the right thing but, as it turns out, you are not. Oops! More prework and evidence might have helped. You'll also have egg on your face and could have just cost the business lots of money.

If you fail to take **ACTION,** you will condemn your business or project to the scrapheap of time. The road to hell is paved with good intentions, so they say. So sort out your project plan and make it happen.

If you fail to get your **TIMINGS** right, you will create inefficiencies, frustration, and will probably lose money. Tasks will slip. And if you ask people to do what they see as the wrong thing at the wrong time, you will encounter resistance. Resistance is not futile, that's why we do it.

If you fail to **TRAIN** your people, then your plans will be sabotaged by people who cannot do what you ask of them and who will not be able to grow themselves at a rate that allows them to deliver any growth to your business. People will be frustrated and will not feel important. Good people will leave while the less able struggle. As the old cliché goes: What if we train our people and they leave? Well, what if we don't train them and they stay?

Failure to **ENCOURAGE** people leads to alienation at work and development and strategic goals not being met. In addition, negativity will seep into the workplace and will be visible to customers. A negative team is a poorly performing team. You also run the risk of sabotage, where people dig their heels in to actively prevent and delay progress (yes, it does happen).

If you fail to **ANNOUNCE** what you are doing, then you risk people putting their own reasons behind your motives. Nobody likes surprises and when people see the action but without knowing the reasons, they have no chance to buy in, no chance to support, or to even realize what is going on. This creates resistance and can even promote fear as people often fantasize about losing their jobs.

If you fail to **REVIEW,** then you are condemning yourself to repeating the same old mistakes again and again. Doing the same thing time after time and expecting a different outcome each time is a first definition of madness.

And if you fail to **SUCCEED,** then celebrate small wins (because they will always be there) and keep trying, keep working, and think about which of the other 14 areas you needed to work at.

What about the "And"?

But what about that small conjunctive in the middle? The word "and." The word "and" is the glue that effortlessly ties everything together. It gives the three words meaning. Without the word "and," the three words BLOOD, SWEAT, TEARS appear nothing more than a list. But when we bring in the conjunctive "and," the three suddenly have cumulated impact, allowing the three to come together in a more powerful way. So, the "and" is more than just a word; it actually means something and pulls the concept together.

To this end, we have devoted a chapter to the "and." So, what is it? In our view, the "and" is the personal strength, power, and dedication that you will bring to your working world when you are at your best. The "and" includes your own mental health and physical well-being, and it includes looking after your family and those around you and finding equal space in your life for all things.

So, read on. Challenge your mind to think creatively about how you can embed these ideas into your everyday thinking, thinking that will help you to define your vision and identify your product, price it correctly, take it to market, get business, make a profit, keep your customers wanting more, motivate and inspire your staff, delight your suppliers, reward your stakeholders and your loved ones, and give yourself a sense of satisfaction and delight in who you are and what you have achieved.

Our Methods

Throughout these books, we employ some old techniques tried and tested since the ancient Greeks and developed further by a multitude of respected gurus, psychologists, organizational development theorists, coaches, management consultants, and successful businessmen and women from around the world. But we also give you new ideas and our latest thinking on some blended approaches which we have used and which we know work. We will give you war stories of where things didn't work and companies got it so wrong—and compare these to where they got it so right and share that best practices with you, giving you the best chance to set up and run your business or team successfully. We will introduce you to some models to help you conceptualize some of the more important areas.

How you use this series of books is up to you. You can read the books cover-to-cover in chapter order or jump directly to the area where you need help today and use it as a standalone chapter without the rest of the book(s) holding you! So, if you just want to target specific areas, then of course you can.

We hope very much that you enjoy "BLOOD, SWEAT, and TEARS" and that you can use it to fuel a wonderful success story.

Steve Elkins-Jarrett and Nick Skinner
London
April 2018

CHAPTER 1

T Is for Training

Are You Training the Right People in the Right Way?

"Train People so they can leave—treat them so they don't want to!"
—Richard Branson

People are hard wired to learn. We learn from the day we are born. Shaping what we learn turns us into the people we are today, and focused learning trains us to cope with situations and events and allows us to do things better, faster, and with more success. Training people at work is all about teaching, coaching, facilitating, and sharing the best ways to do something in a way that allows them to be at their best and to fulfil their potential. It also includes showing others the skills and behaviors needed to carry out tasks or behave in a certain way, so that another person can then do it for themselves without you.

What's Your Training Strategy?

As a leader or manager, you need to decide what your approach is to training. And before we go too far down this line, let's lay our cards on the table:

We believe that training is paramount to your own success and to the success of your business and that if you can only afford to invest in one thing, then invest in your people and the development of their skills. The returns and heightened levels of employee engagement that you can get through good-quality training will prove this to be true.

Many companies throw money at training and tick the box that says training delivered, then sit back and wait for an improvement to happen, but that is not how training works. Training should not be viewed as something that is done to your employees, but rather should be viewed as developing a growth mindset culture of continuous performance improvement, learning, and self-development. Doing this motivates staff, keeps them with you longer, makes them more productive, and they will go the extra mile for you if you invest in them. In thinking about your training strategy, it's worth bearing in mind the 70-20-10 principle. This is a view that training should be 70 percent experiential, 20 percent social learning from peers, and 10 percent formal training, most of which is likely to be externally delivered. In other words, for best results, you need a mixed approach.

A training strategy involves the systematic training and improvement of people within the organization so that they, and the company, can achieve their objectives and both personal and corporate goals. Training strategies vary according to requirements, but important components include:

- Objectives: why are we doing this; what impact do we expect to see; and how does it move us closer toward fulfilling our mission and vision?
- What methods will we use? Considering:
  - Team building and engagement: either within one team if a whole department attends or across several teams if learners come from various teams and departments and learn from each other to gain an understanding of what other teams actually do (especially impactful if you can mix the levels in business so that directors attend with customers facing staff, middle, junior, and senior managers, and supervisors), then all learn together, fostering a team spirit across the whole business.
  - Team development—as above
  - Leadership development (including high-potential leadership)
  - Reflective and Action Learning sets
  - Coaching and mentoring
- Who will receive the training?
  - How do we know what people need? Will it be staff only? Will you include subcontractors or visiting staff, or students?

- Where will we do it and who will lead on this?
    - Can we deliver in-house, will we send people off site, will we employ a learning and development specialist?
- How will we assess the impact?

Plus, of course, how much money are you prepared to put in?

Assessing the Return on Investment (ROI) of Training

It seems reasonable to assume that the amount of money that you dedicate to training earns some form of return. Otherwise why do it? Measuring the return on investment, also known as RoI, is an important factor in many businesses, especially where competition for internal resources is either deeply political, highly competitive, or both. Some businesses and managers are obsessed by RoI. There is a trend to this obsession, in that, in our experience, such attitudes are predominant in businesses that demonstrate a closed mindset to training, fearing that all they are doing by training their people is upskilling someone so they can leave. These are foolish thoughts. The miserable "What if we train our people and they leave?" question should be responded to with "What if we don't train them and they stay?" It's a horrid prospect. We believe that it is important to understand and appreciate the impact that training has on people and your business, but you need to understand that many of these benefits are intangible (like cultural growth, engagement, and happiness).* RoI where used can take many forms from the speed it takes to do something, to the number produced every hour or day. It might be that the impact will be found in growing sales, increased profits, happier staff, time to fill vacancies, average length of time employees stay with you, internal promotions, team scores, customer service score/net promoter scores, waste, and so on. In truth, almost every aspect can be measured and this shows that training pays, now, later, and forever.

---

*Actually, we believe that you can measure these things, but that would take us to a depth of discussion that is beyond the scope of this book. If you are seeking a good book on the power of happiness, then we suggest you read *Flow: The Psychology of Happiness* by Mihaly Csikszentmihalyi.

Establishing Training Needs

Many organizations capture training needs by conducting a Training Needs Analysis (TNA). This process creates a document usually owned by the Human Resources team, and is built upon using data generated from discussions held as part of performance appraisal. A TNA provides information on the training and skills development requirements of all members of each team or business and is a key step in preparing a training plan. A good TNA will identify the gap between current and required levels of knowledge, skills, and aptitude and identify what the general content of training should be. It will form the foundation of a training plan and also give a baseline for the evaluation of it. If managed properly, it will ensure that appropriate and relevant training is delivered. This all sounds ideal, and wonderfully logical. However, in our experience, TNAs tend to be out of date, poorly controlled and even more poorly managed. On top of this, they are often just one person's view of the needs of another. They are well intentioned, but often fail to detect deeper learning needs. Instead, and as a consequence of poorly co-ordinated TNAs, many training initiatives are knee-jerk responses based on the view of one person—"You need to go on a presentation skills course!" In truth, you can determine the needs of individuals in many ways, including TNAs, but the best of these include input from the individuals and their peers, and not just the line manager or someone in central HR. This more detailed understanding of others can be through appraisal through a 360-degree feedback, but also by working closely with these individuals, understanding their needs (See our discussion on the modern applications of Maslow hierarchy in the first volume of this trilogy of Blood, Sweat, and Tears). Another key factor to consider is the individuals own mix of skill/willingness combination (also covered in the "Blood" book), and by helping them be able to do what needs to be done to get actions underway (see the Forcefield exercise in our second book, "Sweat").

To be most effective, a training plan should include—for each person in your business:

- What will be learnt?
- Why?
- By whom?
- When?

- How?
- When will it be complete?
- How will the training be evaluated? What will be the impact on the business and what will be the RoI?

Are You Training the Right People?

Most companies spend 80 percent of their training budget on the top 20 percent of staff[1] and this equates to about 7 percent of the gross turnover spent on training by the top 100 companies in the UK. The rest spent less than 1 percent. The top 20 percent aspect is interesting, for even if you can make a 10 percent difference to the efficiency and performance of this group, you will only increase efficiency by 2 percent. In addition, the average time spent on personal development is 2 weeks in classroom and on courses by the leadership groups, and only 3 to 4 days by most staff. The average spend is over £2,000 per executive per year (the Training Report 2015) and under £15 per staff member per year. But if you spent 80 percent of your training budget on the 80 percent staff and still made a 10 percent difference, it could increase your turnover by 8 percent. After all, your customer-facing staff and fee-earning staff are rarely the executives.

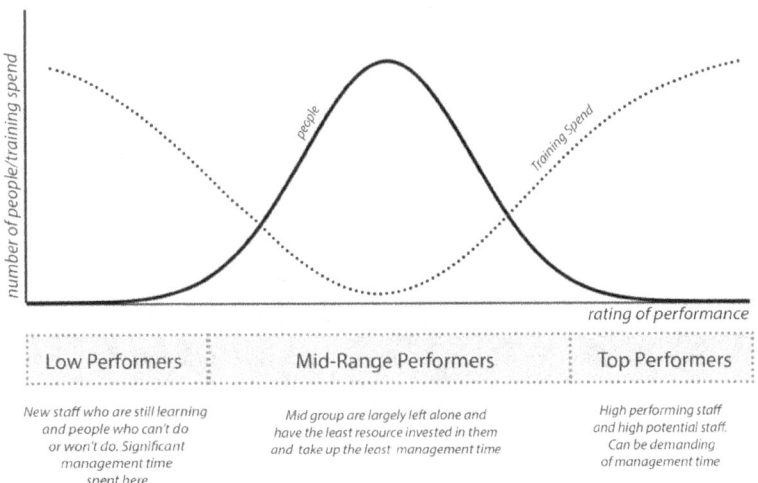

The training spend problem

---

[1]Forbes—Josh Bersin 4th Feb. 2014 www.forbes.com

The illustration shows the typical relationship between performance and training spend. Many organizations show a performance distribution as shown on the diagram. This suggests that somewhere between 10 percent and 20 percent of staff fall into the Low Performance category. These might be new staff who do not yet have the skills to do their job well, or they might be staff with longer service but who cannot, or will not, perform. At the top end of the scale are the 10 percent to 20 percent of staff who fall into the Top Performer category. These are the stars who drive the business on. Generally speaking, it is at these two ends of the performance distribution that organizations spend their training budget. Rather like a classroom teacher, 80 percent of your manager's time is spent dealing with 10 percent of the poorest performers in your team and also the top 10 percent of performers who can be equally demanding. The 80 percent of staff in the middle—the staff who turn up on time, do a good job, cause no issues with managers—are largely forgotten and only get 20 percent of the manager's time and this time is mainly at team meetings, 121s (one-to-ones) (if they get one), and the annual appraisal, and maybe setting daily tasks and longer-term goals, targets, and objectives. This is also the group that often receive the poorest share of the training budget because attention is focused at the low and high ends of the performance scale. Spend at the two ends of the performance scale are higher than in the middle, where greater benefits might accrue. If this is true—and we believe it is—surely companies should reverse this thinking and spend much more of their budget improving skills across the board.

Add to this the belief that most UK companies have that about 80 percent of persons' ability to do a job is directly proportionate to the correct and appropriate behaviors being used and only 20 percent based on the tasks, skills, and abilities of staff;[2] and given the fact that 75 percent of corporate training budget is spent on compulsory and legal training, such as health and safety, first aid, data protection, equal opportunities, diversity, discrimination, and local and national induction, we believe companies are spending their training budgets in the wrong places.

Our belief is quite simple; spend more of your budget on the customer-facing and fee-earning staff and focus it on behavior and understanding oneself and others.

---

[2]https://www.thebalance.com

In four studies on companies that tried this new innovative approach and which we have worked with, we have seen results echoing the following[3,4]:

- 26 percent more revenue per employee
- 40 percent lower staff turnover
- Lower recruitment costs
- Quicker to fill vacancies
- 87 percent better ability to employ the right people for new jobs
- 156 percent better time management of leaders to be strategic and drive the bigger picture
- Lower staff absence (higher attendance); various positive percentages from 2 to 9 percent more staff attending per day than in the previous year
- Higher sales and more upselling up to 20 percent per annum
- Higher staff satisfaction survey scores from 5.7/10 to 7+/10
- Higher NPS (net promoter scores) from customers; a rise from 6 to 7+/10—every company has a unique score, so the worst was 7 and the best over 9
- More repeat business—80 percent customers came back again
- Higher motivation and morale of staff

A lot of companies in the UK talk about competencies in terms of skills, knowledge, and behaviors:

Skills: the physical abilities to carry out a task or a series of tasks to a desired standard.

Knowledge: to know how to do a task or solve something or the mental ability to complete the above tasks well.

Behaviors: the appropriate voice pitch, tone, volume, and content with the right facial mask and body language so that the person they are dealing with can fully understand both what and how they are communicating.

---

[3]Deloitte study 2015/16—www2.deloitte.com millennial survey
[4]Success Profile 2016 http://www.ddiworld.com/products/success-profiles

Companies are spending most of their money on the top 20 percent of staff in leadership and management roles and training these leaders in the skills and knowledge areas and less on behaviors.

We think they should spend most of their money on the 80 percent of staff who are fee earning and customer facing and more on behavior and less on knowledge and skills most of which can be learned on the job using the 70-20-10 method of training delivery.

How Can This Be Done Effectively?

Companies use behavioral profiling tools to get senior staff to understand their behaviors, like Thomas International's DISC, Myers-Briggs MBTI, SDI, Insights, and LIFO and include 360s, teams and Saville and Holdsworth's OPQ, NEO's Big-5, and SPECTRUM. In the UK, Chartered Institute of Personnel and Development (CIPD) and the British Psychological Society (BPS) say over 70 percent of all companies use psychometrics and we completed over 4 million tests nationally in the UK, with an average spend of over £100 per profile; this could be worth millions spent on just 20 percent of all working adults.

In our practice, we have settled on the use of the SPECTRUM model and profile and suggest it can support training and development in the following ways:

- By profiling staff before joining to see how closely they match your values.
- By profiling new job roles before they are filled to suggest best behavioral fit.
- By giving all staff a model of behavior with common language and a tool they can all use to understand themselves and others in minutes, meaning they can relate to colleagues and customers in seconds and better deal with stress, pressure, and conflict.
- By enabling managers to talk to their staff in their language to motivate them better.
- By allowing staff to relate to customers and pick up on upsell opportunities.

- By allowing competencies to be described using behaviors in a common language so that everyone knows what needs to be done and how a job should be carried out.
- By giving all staff (not just top 20 percent) access to a better understanding of their behavior and how it impacts on others.
- By acknowledging that we are taught as children to treat others how WE want to be treated, but this is wrong! We have to treat others how THEY want to be treated.

The key thing with training is that whatever you chose to "impose" from the center, you must also allow people to pursue their own goals. You must allow them to maintain a growth mindset where the phase "I can't" is soon overcome. Whatever method you use, once you have established the training needs of a person or a group of people, you have the responsibility to then deliver that solution through:

1. Learning on the job from others who are great at their jobs—mentoring and teamwork. How do others do it and can they show me? Who are your champions? May not be managers and leaders.
2. Learning from online materials; written, spoken, and video, CD ROMs, and books; both e-books and hard copies based on the preference of the learners. Take a learning styles survey at www.evaluationstore.com to find your learning style. Most people enjoy watching media, listening to, or reading something about their jobs or area of interest. Plus, this is cheaper and can be done in the employees' own time.
3. Learning with support from a coach who watches you work and gives you feedback on your style, behaviors, and techniques and helps you to make small improvements. Like making a more impactful presentation by him/her watching you and directing the way you might do it differently, change your voice pitch, tone, or volume, restructure it, use more pictures, be more animated, etc. The most expensive, but in our opinion the best and most effective, training is 121.
4. Attending training courses, college, universities, and business schools etc., here you have a whole industry at your feet and an

established network of learning establishments that will be only too happy to squeeze one more on their course. These courses can be "tool box talks" for 1 hour, "skill bite" sessions for 2 to 4 hours, or 1 to 2 days courses or even 1 week, 1 month, or block release to a college for 3 months at a time over 2 to 3 years, and so on. Great as you are with other learners and can gain as much from them as you do the courses.

5. Learning from self-discovery from being inquisitive and asking questions how, why, where, and what? Can I do this better or differently? When Edison invented the light bulb, he didn't try to make a candle burn brighter, he looked at a new way to light a room. Allowing people to devote certain percentages of their time to pursuing their own curiosity at work can reap substantial benefits and is personally rewarding. It can create innovative new approaches to complex work problems and create new commercial or process opportunities where none were previously thought to exist. Note that this is the cheapest and is highly effective, but your culture must support it. As a leader or manager this also requires the most trust.

6. Sharing best practice inside your organization or outside learning from other companies. Is it possible that a construction company could learn something from an investment bank or vice versa? Such cross-referenced activities and inquiries can accelerate learning in quantum leaps, allowing us to learn from the best behaviours and methods of others.

Learning on the Job from Others

On-the-job training , also known as OJT, is one of the strongest training methods because it is planned, organized, and conducted at the employee's workplace and as such has an unrivalled validity. On-the-job training gives people confidence and allows new trainees to be inducted efficiently and quickly into the company.

Self-esteem, high yield and professionalism are always high in those organizations that employ a logical and reasonable on-the-job training program. Such approaches empower staff to apply their new skills. This form of training is usually the principal method used for augmenting employee skills and escalating output and efficiency. It is mainly suitable for developing expertise distinctive to an employee's job, chiefly in those positions whose work is relatively easy to learn and which requires locally owned equipment and facilities. By looking at the key outputs of your job, as identified in the first volume in this trilogy, you can easily see which outputs require the training first and need higher productivity, less waste, more efficiency, and so on. You can measure the time it takes to produce or carry out a task and see it improve after training and over time.

Learning can be accelerated where a nominated expert is involved. An expert should be assigned to each employee involved in on-the-job training to make it successful. All these experts; or champions as we also like to call them, are the best persons you have at that task and may not be a manager and may even be several different members of staff. These people have significant relevant knowledge and a positive attitude. They are accountable and responsible for carefully planning the training and also conducting it effectively. On-the-job training is one of numerous ways by which a company might opt to impart the knowledge and skills its employees require. Compare being taught by the best painter and decorator the firm has on its books, to copy and watch the tricks of the trade first hand to being taught in college by a lecturer who has not worked as a painter or decorator for some years and it is in the classroom environment. Yes, he will learn how to do but not as well as fast or with the techniques that are not "in the book." Your staff members with high skill and high willingness are great for this role, and even high-skilled and low-willingness staff can have their mojo restored by asking them to serve others in this way.

Learning Online

In recent years, there has been a massive growth in online learning, with much content being "gamified" to make it more engaging. The main attraction for this is the low cost with which these packages can be sustained, and without doubt there is some excellent content being built and larger companies are offering certain standard packages online. Very often, these include mandatory courses central to the businesses' key activities. For instance, if you join a construction company, you might well be offered online training in health and safety, manual handling, handling of dangerous materials, etc. Some businesses go the whole hog and attempt to move their full learning catalog online. In our minds, this removes the human aspect from the process and moves training toward a "tick box" philosophy. Thus, online training should be part of your offering but not the entire sum of your package.

The material available covers a variety of programs and courses from traditional four-year universities to completely online career colleges. For younger learners, many colleges and universities have begun to accept credits/points earned via free massive open online courses (MOOCs), the most recent advance in online education. Free online courses such as these can help learners fulfill general education requirements at little to no cost and can give credits that count toward other qualifications.

Online learning is great for people with family commitments and also suits the changing demographics of the workplace, plus it's more carbon friendly. Why fly me to Dubai for a week of training when I can do the whole course from my lounge while still wearing my pyjamas? Plus, there is a side effect to online learning; it keeps me computer literate, and might even grow my skills. This is an important consideration in many manual industries where people do not sit at a computer all day. The massive growth in the use of mobile devices also helps here, with people intuitively picking up how to use new technology thanks to some very clever people working in the user experience departments of Apple, Samsung, and other technology businesses.

Learning from Coaching and Mentoring

Getting support from a coach is, in our opinion, unparalleled and powerful. The great benefit of coaching is that you are very likely to see quick, positive results as an outcome. This is because coaching is participative, and people tend to learn and adopt new habits more easily when they are actively engaged in the learning process. It is also very personal and goes deep. As soon as a coaching session ends, you can implement a new practice. Coaching is very similar to learning on the job, but we feel it is more likely to be a behavioral change rather than getting better at a task. In the business world, there is executive coaching and life coaching which is about understanding yourself, understanding others, and teams being able to influence and persuade and get your message across better. Growing into a new role would be one area. Ironically in business, employers usually promote the best person at doing the job into the manager's shoes, thus removing the best worker from the production line and now asking him or her to manage others while having no experience or knowledge in managing or supervising others in behavior, motivation, or dealing with conflict and stress (all skills you will certainly need to lead others). Sometimes the best potential manager may not be the best at his current job; if you took the top leading goal scorer off the field of play and made him the manager, what might happen?—Well, the team might stop scoring so many goals, lose matches, and the stressed-out new manager then uses excessive behaviors to try and motivate them into being better. The same happens in sales; the multimillion-dollar deal maker gets promoted to be national sales manager, he stops selling, his customers are unhappy, the sales dip, the directors make redundancies, and then dismiss the new sales manager for poor performance. So be weary of this and use coaching to get your employees right and ready for any promotions before they step into the new role.

Coaching improves performance, enabling self-doubt to be overcome and goals to be achieved. It promotes ownership of outputs and improves attitudes toward personal learning and development. People who have had a coach are evangelical about the benefits of coaching and are often the first to suggest coaching as an option for others. Coaching develops self-awareness and the ability to handle negative feedback, and, because it is behavioral in nature, it goes deep and allows some fundamental realignments to occur. Many people experience their "eureka moment" in coaching, whether that takes the form ofgreater clarity in rolesand objectives, personal goals or ambitions or how to forge the best personal interactions in the workplace.

Coaching also offers significant benefits to the organization by realizing the potential of people and sparking their engagement and motivation. Through the ability of people to hit their targets, it grows performance and builds a culture of learning and success.

The tricky part can be the selection of the coach. Because of the nature of the relationship, you must be certain that the chemistry between the individual and the coach is "right." Any coach worth their salt will give you an introductory session to see if that chemistry is right. After all, they don't want to be seated there in a rapport vacuum any more than you do. You'll also need to decide what form of accreditation you want to see from your coach. Some are academically qualified and might lack the business skills you seek. Others might be too commercially focused and not academic enough. It's a personal thing. And one last thing on coaching. Coaching is not therapy (although some people can experience it as such). Your coach is there to support you in your work-based learning. From time to time, this will involve crossing the threshold into your private life, but a good coach should know how far that conversation should be allowed to go. If you need a therapist or if you think you are ill, seek a specialist and not a coach.

Learning from Training Courses

Training courses are useful ways of developing skill sets in a number of people in one session. As such, they are considered value for money and can create great outcomes provided you can partner with a creative training provider. Productivity usually increases when a company implements training courses; they can improve performance across a range of areas, not just the direct topic of that particular course. By investing to training for your staff, you are likely to see improvements in competitiveness, morale, customer satisfaction, cross team working, communications, willingness, and tie management. You can also see reductions in turnover and absenteeism, recruitment, workplace accidents and grievances, and industrial relations style incidents. Training also makes a company more attractive to potential new recruits who seek to improve their skills and the opportunities associated with those new skills.

The question remains as to what courses should you offer? This of course will depend on the training strategy and any work that may have been done on a training needs analysis. Over the years, we have found these topics to be the most commonly requested:

Developing your strategy with all or some of the employees involved
Developing a strategy—directors only

Leadership and management skills

Presentation skills

Coaching for managers

Team development

Team building

Problem solving

Change

Succession planning

Induction and onboarding

Leading safely

Behavioral safety

Networking

Performance management process

Basic understanding of HR and Employment Law for all managers

High-potential development and talent spotting and management

Assessment centers

Finance for non-accountants

Project management

Negotiation skills

Unconscious bias training

Interviewing skills

Well-being and mindfulness—managers understanding stress

Sales and upselling

Getting to Yes

Getting past No

Report writing

In addition, the role of simulation exercises, business war-games, and decision-making games and facilitated workshops that were discussed in our earlier volumes are also great for upskilling people and sharing best practice. In fact, these can often create much more positive outcomes than simply "sending someone on a course." Any engaging training provider or facilitator should be able to create a bespoke learning environment to target at specific need. And if they can't, then contact us because we certainly can.

Learning from Self-Discovery or Reflection

Sociologist Jack Mezirow famously said that "A defining condition of being human is that we have to understand the meaning of our experience."

Reflecting on work enhances its meaning. Hold a mirror up to my face and I have to study who I am, warts and all. Reflection is a powerful tool, giving us the chance to look back on events and contextualize them somewhere in our understanding of events.

Reflective learning can be fuelled through learning sets. Self-managed learning (SML) is an independent and interdependent process of learning in which individuals are the key controllers of their own learning and the prime dictators of their own outcomes. Sometimes seen as part of an organization's overall training and development strategy, SML is not a training event in the traditional sense of the term. There is no common syllabus or timetable, but is characterized by an emphasis on the individuals to identify their own learning needs and follow this through in a live organizational context. The learning aims can be varied, allowing theoretical as well as very precise skills to be pursued. We've grown our own skills through this enlightened and enabled approach and it is highly recommended.

A key component and driver of learning in the concept of SML is the learning group, normally four to six people strong and often created as part of a learning cohort on a high-potential leadership or management skills program. The group is the primary place where each person negotiates their contract for learning and then carries out actions and reflections on their obligations, so people become accountable to themselves and to each other. This shared responsibility drives deep commitment. Groups meet periodically (with a frequency dictated by the group itself) and the format of such sessions normally includes time for each individual to discuss or present their progress to date with their chosen learning topic in a forum where other members of the group are encouraged to comment, provide feedback, and suggest direction. Each member of the group will typically be given a fair share of "air time" within the group to discuss their own case, and is expected to play an active part in the feedback, encouragement, and direction offered to other members of the learning set. Discussions should be confidential, candid, honest, and objective. Learning groups like this are about individuals taking control of what and why they learn, and how this happens. A successful group will offer a good balance of pressure, respect, support, and direction, building on its own uniqueness, both real and perceived, to encourage members to try out new ideas, provide suitable feedback—negative if necessary—to keep its members on track to achieve their prestated aims. Individuals may also build a useful peer network that they will continue to draw upon after the learning has been completed.

SML can take place without the learner leaving the workplace, bringing the learning contract directly into contact with the "real" organization and working environment. This reality gives authenticity to the learning process and thus the individual's job development and learning path become inexorably intertwined.

Reflection in this way involves linking a current experience to previous learnings (a process called *scaffolding*), drawing forth cognitive and emotional information from several sources. To reflect, we must act upon and process the information, synthesizing and evaluating the data. In the end, reflecting also means applying what we've learned to contexts beyond the original situations in which we learned something.

Learning from Sharing Best Practice

Facilitated workshops (described elsewhere), interactive courses (described earlier), and learning sets (also described earlier) offer opportunities to share best practice. Best practice is the change for people to work together with their peers and to learn from each other. Establishing a corporate knowledge sharing strategy, promoting a culture of knowledge sharing, and leveraging learning technology to execute these efforts can drive organizational growth and help reach positive business outcomes. SBP (also sometimes known as Communities of Practice) sessions come in a variety of guises and so can be a formal part of training or run separately as informal events targeted around a problem. Sharing knowledge is an essential ingredient for business prosperity; however, a recent survey by Brandon Hall Group found that only one-third of organizations have a defined corporate knowledge sharing strategy. The study also discovered that only 20 percent of companies believe their knowledge sharing efforts are effective. You don't need a big budget, but to get value from these sessions you are well advised to employ a specialist facilitator who will hold the boundaries and encourage contribution. Sharing best practice is as old as civilization itself. Consider the following story of Ugg and Thugg.

The Neanderthals sat huddled around the fire. The soft orange light reflected from the walls of the large cave in which they were gathered, giving an eerie light to proceedings. From the walls of the cave the dull handprints and paintings of the top mammoth hunters from all ancestry hung over the group, reminding them of just why they were here.

Ugg grunted first. He grunted of how he and his team of hunters had worked all day to corner the great mammoth whose carcass now filled their bellies. It was the first time they'd eaten mammoth in many moons. The other hunters sat and listened as Ugg told the tale of how he, newly returned to the community from sabbatical work with the tribe on the other side of the stream, demonstrated how he had used his new "cat-a-pult" process to maximum effect to bring down the giant beast. They listened in awe. "Cat-a-pult." What a strange device. The hunters glanced uneasily at each other as Ugg handed round the new device for them all to look at. They poked it and grunted excitedly.

The mighty Thugg grunted back loudly. He queried Ugg on his exploits. What was this weird-looking "cat-a-pult" device that Ugg had used? How had it made him approach the hunt in a different and more successful way? What lessons could he share? Could Ugg show them all how to use it?

Ugg shifted uncomfortably in his loincloth and picked a gristly piece of mammoth flesh from between his few remaining teeth. Thugg was a powerful caveman who certainly knew what he was grunting about. He'd been the community's most successful mammoth bagger of recent times. What he didn't know about mammoth bagging could be smeared on the walls of the largest cavern in the valley. Why should he be interested in what Ugg had to say? Didn't he know it all already?

But thanks to his ever-growing prefrontal cortex, Thugg knew that he could learn from Ugg. Ugg had been to the wacky tribe across the stream, he'd seen how they used that new-fangled catapult thing-a-ma-jig, and he'd brought that knowhow back to the group. Sending him there had been worthwhile after all. If the hunters whose faces he could see now in the dim glow of the fire could master this new technology, then there was hope for the tribe after all. If they could share Ugg's expertise, then this community could be the greatest mammoth bagging group of all time, securing complete market domination within even the shortest planning horizon . . . maybe they could make a better catapult capable of bringing down even bigger mammoths . . . profits would soar, and he might get promotion to the Board . . .

You get the message.

Working and talking together to share new and best practices isn't new. Ugg and Thugg did it as part of an intuitive process millions of years ago. That intuition remains strong with us today. We know it makes sense to share our stories and new ways of working with our colleagues and yet so few of us manage to squeeze in any time to do this. Result? Our mammoth bagging techniques are outdated, impractical, and we are seldom at our best. In short, we are not all using the catapult. The moral of the story? Schedule time for your team to come together to share stories. By sharing experiences, they will share new thinking, generate new ideas, and will soon be sharing best practice.

You know it makes sense.

Remember These Golden Rules about Training

Train people so they can leave, treat them so they don't.

Training must be meaningful and relate to a measurable job/task improvement

RoIs are hard to measure and might be wrong

Training should align people to their personal goals and ambitions

Take a balanced approach: 70/20/10 is pretty good

Coaching works!

Don't just throw money at it—target it

Remember, 80 percent is behavioral; so focus on that bit

CHAPTER 2

E Is for Encouragement

Can You Give Encouragement to Others so That They Can Be at Their Best?

"Encouragement is telling someone that they can achieve anything if they put their minds to it—the only thing stopping them is their lack of imagination and will power."

—Mike Smith of Manskill Associates

Encouraging people is the action of giving them support, confidence, or hope. The intention is to motivate and inspire people to succeed, even in the darkest of days when this is needed more than others. This chapter explores some ideas around encouragement from two perspectives. Firstly, the encouragement of others; what motivates people and how you can press the right buttons to inspire great performance? Secondly, we'll look at how you can make sure that you surround yourself with the right people, and the right ways of working to make sure that you get the encouragement and support that you need to keep going at those times when you most need that vital boost.

Encouraging Others

Dan Pink is a man who knows a thing or two about motivation. His TED talk on intrinsic and extrinsic motivators has, at the time of writing, 19.7 million views. You've probably seen it, and if you haven't watched it yet, then you definitely should.

Pink argues very powerfully that the traditional method of carrot-and-stick rewards is no longer suitable for most white-collar jobs in the 21st century. We know that when it comes down to what motivates people at work, money comes low down the list. In fact, it most surveys of the role that money plays in motivating people it is normally somewhere between 6th and 8th. Pink states that separate research carried out by Behavioral Economist Dan Ariely, Sam Glucksberg, and the London School of Economics shows that for more complex jobs, the use of financial incentives can have a negative impact on performance. His excellently delivered presentation of just under 20 minutes sums up perfectly what we have also experienced in many of the organizations with which we have worked. "*Traditional notions of management are great if you want compliance, but if you want engagement then self-direction works better.*"

What is meant by self-direction? Pink argues this comes down to three things: Autonomy (the urge to direct our own lives), Mastery (the desire to get better and better at something that matters), and Purpose (the yearning to do what we do in the service of something larger than ourselves). In the terms we have already addressed in this book, it is about giving people what they need to climb the pyramid of work needs that we looked at in our chapter on leadership in the first volume of this trilogy. If you want to encourage people to perform at their best, you must give them this space.

Pink goes on to talk about a concept known as ROWE, which we have come across in previous books and which stands for Results Only Work Environment. As its name suggests, this is a way of working that allows people the flexibility they need to work in the way that they want. And this is something that we see many organizations now wishing to support. It does away with the 9 to 5 rat race and makes work more fulfilling.

There are some other, much simpler things that can be done to encourage others and to cheer them on. Firstly, never underestimate the power of a simple "thank you." Lack of appreciation is often stated as a reason why people leave jobs. I know that I have had many conversations with people who have left one company to go to another just because they felt that they weren't appreciated in their last job. Again, we appreciate and say "thank you" as an enabler that allows people to feel worthy and have a sense of belonging and connection. The feeling of being valued and appreciated is enough for some people, and, speaking in terms of those individuals who have a "green" SPECTRUM profile, the need to feel appreciated is a massive driver. After all, these are people whose focus is on making sure that YOU are OK. But whatever their SPECTRUM profile colour, a "thank you" never hurts anyone and is good manners.

At its basic level, a "thank you" is a form of positive feedback, an appreciation of something that has been done. Feedback is a powerful tool in business, as it helps us to develop, direct, and even control people. Effective feedback that is clear and focused and given regularly, even when it is negative in nature, can still be helpful and encouraging. There are four basic types of feedback: positive, negative, developmental, and productive. Positive feedback such as "You're great" is nice to get but can be shallow, appear insincere or, if not supported with evidence, not really that helpful. But it can be encouraging. There are times in the working week when your team will just need to hear a few words of encouragement, especially if they are working hard to meet a deadline or nail an impossible task. That's fine. Be liberal, but not too liberal. There is a balance to be struck here. If you suddenly go into the office tomorrow and start praising everybody for everything they do, then your comments will have the opposite effect. Praise should be given when it is due, but to make it genuine you should be honest about when it is deserved, with a slight balance in favor of the person who has made the effort! Praising in public is also a good move.

Negative feedback can be damaging if delivered in the wrong way and should certainly not be delivered in public, where it can be even more damaging. It is far more preferable to use developmental or productive feedback. The difference between developmental and productive feedback escaped me for many of my early years, despite how much I had been told about it then one day I was sitting at a school parents' evening with my daughter, listening to her Geography teacher. The teacher gave Katie a great piece of developmental feedback when he said "Katie, you're a great student and your attention to detail in class is superb, but you need to get better marks in the tests." Now then, there are a few things here. Firstly, the use of the word "but." As a general rule, the word "but" is an unhelpful word to be used in feedback conversations as it completely invalidates everything that was said before it, and puts the emphasis on the bit after the "but." There is a great saying for this: "Everything before the 'but' is bulls*t." Remember that when giving feedback. The other thing the teacher had said that was good but which was spoiled by the "but" was that he'd started with a piece of good positive feedback. She was a great student with superb attention to detail. That was nice to hear, so it would have been nice to be able to enjoy that on its own before the "but." The second part of his sentence though, was the bit that I picked up on: "You need to get better marks in the test" was a statement of a developmental need. The message was clear, she needed to get better marks. But while that feedback was *developmental* it wasn't actually *productive*, because it left Katie with no idea how she was supposed to achieve the development goal that was stated. What does she need to do to get better marks? Write more? Include more diagrams? Say please? To be productive, the teacher would have needed to say something like "we now need to get your test marks up by including some images of plate tectonics." Bingo. Katie would have now had a much clearer idea of what she needed to do to improve. The feedback was both *developmental* (it stated the need) and *productive* (it gave an idea of how). And therefore, more useful. Let's compare again the two instances of feedback in this example. In the first instance, the teacher said "Katie, you're a great student and your attention to detail in class is superb, but you need to get better marks in the tests," while the more encouraging version might have gone more like "Katie, you're a great student and your attention to detail in class is superb. We now need to get your test marks up by including some images of plate tectonics."

Hopefully, you can see that the second version is much more encouraging and is going to leave the other person feeling more confident. Incidentally, I did give the teacher the feedback about the conversation which was positively received, and I am pleased and proud to say that Katie got a great pass in her exam.

It's worth adding that from a developmental perspective (and through the eyes of a coach), an even more helpful approach is not to provide the solution directly but instead to ask a question. This depends on the state of knowledge and understanding of the person about their own situation, but in a workplace feedback conversation with a coaching style, it would be smart to ask the other person what they think needed to be different. After all, they are a professional with their own views of the world.

Hence, to adjust that example for a work conversation after a presentation, you might say something like "Katie, that was a great presentation and the data insights really helped me to understand the situation. How was it for you?" Notice that this asks the other person to reflect on the situation and allows you to listen to their responses. It gives no sign that you have an opinion on what needed to be different. Of course, where the conversation goes after that is up to you, but it is quite likely that you will be able to follow up with "What might you do differently next time round?" which is a great question from a developmental perspective. We will look more at delivering feedback and some models you may find helpful for the delivery of it in a later chapter.

Encouraging Yourself

You are much more likely to see the good in others when you recognize the good in yourself, so your own self-motivation is a factor that must not be overlooked. As you move through life, you form a perception about who you are, and the difference you make to the world. This perception of yourself is called self-esteem, and it shapes many aspects of your life, from the type of work that you do, to the quality of your friends, and your desire and ability to lead and encourage others. Positive self-esteem is critical to mental health and the ability to relate well to others. By strengthening your self-esteem, you can increase contentment in relationships and in your wider life and enjoy greater emotional health of all family members. Your level of self-esteem reflects the strength of your belief in your own abilities and your own worthiness. When you approve of and respect yourself, you'll present yourself confidently to the world in a way that says you're capable, likable, and successful. And other people will likely approve of and respect you, too! This type of personal belief attracts others to you, and it enhances your ability to influence and relate to others. The higher you build your self-esteem without becoming arrogant, the greater your people skills are likely to be.

Conversely, feeling bad about yourself and engaging in critical self-talk can damage your ability to influence and relate to the people around you. They may respect you less and feel wary about working with you. In short, you can't hold others in high regard if you don't value yourself.

The paradox of healthy self-esteem is that we often need someone else to validate ourselves as worthy. We need the support of others and to receive feedback. This is one of the reasons why it is so important to give feedback to people who work with you and why it is important that you yourself receive feedback. Seeking feedback at work through colleagues, managers, or other workers is helpful, but even more powerful is the support and encouragement you can get from your family and friends.

Challenging Critical Self-Talk

The primary focus for people with low self-esteem is often on themselves and what they can do to preserve the small amount of self-worth they do have. Because of this, there's often not much left over for developing good relationships with others. This is why it's so important for us to challenge critical self-talk and to send ourselves positive and reassuring messages, rather than critical ones. Some great ways to challenge negative self-talk include taking care of your physical self by making sure you eat, sleep, exercise, and stay healthy, seek the occasional "quick win" and enjoy the feeling of success that comes with it. You can also reward yourself with compliments, treats, and take time off work for yourself. Do things that make you feel good, make a list of your successes, and display signs of your achievements and best moments. Photos and objects are especially good for this.

Don't criticize yourself and take time to reflect on lessons learned. And remember above all to be fair to yourself. It's OK to fail (because that's where we learn the most) and no one can be successful all the time.

Using SPECTRUM to Encourage Others

As with so many areas, we can use the SPECTRUM tool to help us think about motivation and encouragement.

To encourage people with a predominantly red profile . . . give them autonomy, allow them to make decisions and take responsibility and accountability for their actions. Let them be competitive, risk takers who will want to succeed, but be careful you don't give them too much rope. You must keep the final decision and always know what they are up to.

To encourage blue . . . give them advanced warnings of what you want them to in writing and future pace any changes so that there is no shock. Give them the time and space to be careful, check their work for errors and they love systems, policies, and procedures to follow and by the book—so let them. Don't ask them to take risks or be impulsive.

To encourage green . . . ask, don't tell. Sell ideas, don't push, involve them in discussions and allow them to add value and seek better ways to do something. They like people and are team members and make great reps and supervisors. Ask them to be involved in high-quality projects that are meaningful and important and give them feedback often as they won't ask for it.

To encourage yellow . . . let them be the center of attention, middle of everything, involvement, chance to shine or look good, good at customer service, sales, and marketing. Innovative and creative, so if you want a new look or a different way to do something, ask them. Love gadgets and new technology, so let them have a go with new stuff first.

What Can You Do?

Here are some ideas from us for what you can do to help motivate and encourage people at work.

Ask Questions

Having a conversation with people where you are genuinely interested in their responses builds self-esteem for the person to whom the questions are directed. If you are at a loss as to what motivates people, their passions are a great start. But you might not be able to see these from outside, and your own mindset might skew your thoughts. Instead, ask questions and learn more about people. Do not fall into the error of asking, "What are you passionate about" and taking what they say at face value. Look for body language signs that reinforce their stated passion. Ask for their views. Maybe start with asking how things could be done better around here. Respond with further questions to explore. The phrase, "Tell me more about that" or works well to open up the conversation further. Have several conversations like this, and as trust develops, you will find out what motivates people without having to ask.

Involve

People will support what they have helped to create and they will value it more, meaning that they will work harder to make it succeed and feel more passionate about it. Things we create by ourselves or with others have more value. Just look at how much you value your own kids against other people's kids. The same is true for giving wings to our ideas. For major and minor changes, go further than asking for advice and opinions; involve people in analysis and the design of solutions and look for ways of involving people. Involve them in the analysis to create solutions and they will own the solution alternatives. Involve them in the design of the implementation and they will own the outcome.

Let Go—Delegate More

Giving people more autonomy in their work constantly appears as a key driver of motivation. Think what it is that you, as the manager, can let go of and pass to your subordinates. Not only will this help them develop their skills, but it also allows you to focus upward onto more strategic tasks and activities. If 10 managers in your business can successfully delegate 10 percent of their activities then you've suddenly found a whole new manager! This additional responsibility is likely to be seen as an expression of confidence in their ability which will motivate them to step up. Use delegation techniques to ensure that the transfer of expertise is completed. When delegating, state clearly what is expected and establish a standard for completion that is mutually understood. Check expectations and allow them to ask questions. Delegate the authority. Do not double check them as routine. At the beginning of delegation, monitor their output as part of an agreed standard of handing over the work. Be available to help and guide as appropriate.

Delegation and letting go the one thing that people find hardest to do. That's because it involves deep levels of trust.

Communicate

Uncertainty causes anxiety, and anxious people will not perform at their best. When you are anticipating change, let people know what your intentions are. When we use the word communicate here, we primarily mean talking. Talk to others more. Tell them the goal. Tell them the rationale. Tell them the consequences and timing of what you intend to do. Tell them the consequences and timing of doing nothing. Tell them the process by which things will happen. Tell them how to find out more information. Tell them how to make sure their comments and thoughts are to be included. Let them ask questions. Listen to what they think. Listen to what they would rather do. Listen to their aspirations. Listen to how changing things impacts them.

Give Thanks

Appreciate achievements in public. Even those who shun the limelight will appreciate being commended in a low-key way in public. Be specific. Do not say, "I just want to commend Jess for the great job she is doing." Say instead, "I want to commend and thank Jess for going out of her way to help our customer stay in business. Jess not only came in on Saturday morning when the customer called in a panic, but she personally delivered the part on her way home. She did not have to do that but by choosing to do so, she has helped us all get a reputation for superior service." Nobody is left in doubt as to what behavior, with what consequences, is being commended. It is this precise behavior which will be reinforced.

Reprimand in Private

Embarrassing people in public will demotivate them and others. Reprimanding in a constructive and private manner will motivate. As with the "thank you" above, reprimand as soon as possible after the event and be as specific about the behavior which is unacceptable and the rationale as to why. Be specific about the consequences of repeating the behavior. Ask the person what they think about it and how they think they can best stop the behavior. Work together to eliminate the unacceptable. Note when this happens and commend them.

If the reprimand does not work, use performance appraisal to help you set targets and work on a plan for improvement. This does not have to wait until annual appraisal, your joint efforts are far more likely to work if tackled now, and if tackled honestly. It might be a difficult conversation, but without it things are unlikely to improve.

Support Learning

The ability to get better at work and improve skills is a big motivator. Create a culture that supports learning and development to enable people to build on their strengths and help eliminate their weaknesses. Encourage sharing of ideas to promote learning and critical assessment of how things are done. Identify, appreciate, and build people's strengths, especially those who have weaknesses they are working on. As described in the previous chapter, use all resources at your disposal you can afford. Not only use coaching and training but ask people to train and coach others. Nothing makes people realize their true strengths and weaknesses more than when they are asked to teach. Nothing builds self-esteem like being successful at teaching someone else well and watching their behavior change.

Reward

Reward your staff and yourself often and randomly—random rewards motivate people more than an annual salary increase—that is why fruit machines and penny slot work—random rewards. That little rewards triggers chemical releases in our brain that really do make us feel good. Also a salary increase in for ever on your books and random reward is paid out a profit once every now and gain. There is a company in the UK in the top 10 of best employers and they give inflation raises to most employees annually, they give monthly bonuses to those who hit their targets paid for the increased sales and profits, and they also do a monthly draw for a random employee to win—cash, a weekend away, a holiday, a meal for the family in a restaurant, and so on—this is not based on performance, but is the luck of the draw. (Without the employees knowing, the winner's name is not put in again until a year later!).

Think

Think about what motivates each employee and reward them individually—use Maslow and SPECTRUM to assess whether employee 1 would rather have an enhanced pension, job security, healthcare, a bonus, a holiday, more quality time off, extra holiday, to work from home once a week, to arrive later than everyone else but go home later or vice versa, to have a transparent, fairly applied, equitable league table of your most productive employees at the top, to have an employee of the week or month. To give out certificates and medals in public. It will really make a difference to each employee if you know what makes them tick.

We have found that acting with clarity and honesty will help to counter many rumors that quickly circulate when change is in the air. Being responsible, having the competency and authority to do your job with the trust and support of your colleagues, superiors, and subordinates is a most powerful motivator. Find something, even the smallest thing that an individual can actually be responsible for and you will be on the road to a motivated workforce.

Finally, nothing motivates like success. A team that can work together and build a strong track record of performance will motivate itself through its own results. This team can fly and they encourage and support themselves to be great. As someone once said, "Managing the A team is easy, it's managing the B team that's hard."

Remember These Golden Rules of Motivation

Money is a poor motivator.

You can motivate, inspire, and encourage others just through your own actions.

Motivators are personal—what motivates you might not motivate others. SPECTRUM can help.

Well-delivered feedback can be motivational. Poorly delivered feedback demotivates.

The more you let go, the more space you give for others to step up.

A simple "Thank You" goes a long way.

CHAPTER 3

A Is for Announcements

Can You Announce and Present?

"In the tradition of shocking announcements, who should we leak it to first?"

—Peter Mandelson

Clear communication allows others to understand and engage with your idea. Through clear communication, you can engage and inspire others. Inspiration (quite literally, the breathing of life into something) places a fire in the belly of others that they will use to drive better outcomes. Inspiring others through good communication motivates them to succeed and to share common beliefs. Great communications also provide clarity and reduce the likelihood of misunderstandings and confusion. We know that people make up themselves what they don't hear directly. Therefore, if you want to avoid your workplace or market being rife with fantasy and wrong perceptions, then you must create the right perceptions and convey the clear picture. The question is "how do you do this." As of 2018, there are so many possible new communications channels that we could use and yet we are losing our ability to use our oldest and most trusted. The hypothesis is simple: modern day technology is reducing the human ability to communicate effectively. If you need to exercise to keep the muscles of your body fit, then surely you need to exercise the muscles you use to communicate with others in the same way. But here we are in the 21st century, using radio, TV, movies, CDs, MP3 and MP4, streaming, computers, laptops, tablets, and smart phones so that we are as humans in receive mode and not so much in send mode. We are listening to and watching stuff more and more, but less today than it was 100 years ago when we were using as send mode: eyes, mouth, voice box, and body language.

Effective communication can only happen when the other person receives the message that you intended to send them, and acknowledges to you that they have understood it. To be an effective communicator, we need to send our behaviors out without ambiguity or confusion or the receiver will be confused.

Is it possible that the invention of modern technological devices, all designed to speed up and make communication easier, is in fact making us lazy and allowing muscles to become atrophied and dormant as time goes on?

I genuinely believe that for two people or more to communicate effectively, we need to see their eyes. We use minute muscle movements in the eyes and face to communicate with each other and even pupil size is affected by eye contact, especially in attraction. Our body language is a huge part of the way we communicate. Lastly, our voices which are key is about chosen vocabulary; content and more importantly the pitch, tone, and volumes used are clearly vital components to effective communication—a study carried out by "On how things are said?" Voice Tone, Voice Intensity, Verbal Content, and Perceptions of Politeness written by Laplante and Ambady, Harvard University, in 2003 proved this beyond all reasonable doubt.

Our theory is that as technology has become "better" in helping us communicate more quickly and effectively using this technology that we as human beings are becoming less effective at face-to-face communication and this results in miscommunication, misunderstood communication, or confusion. Here are some observed instances.

Picture a family all sit down in a restaurant and all take out their smart phones, ask for the Wi-fi code, and then spend 10 minutes at least, not mentally in the room, and certainly not looking at or interacting with each other! No verbal communication at all. Picture two teenagers talking to each other outside a shop and no eye contact made at all as they are fixated with the screens on their mobile phones—they are mumbling at each other in a low-frequency slur of words and sound bites, and they are not moving—they are static. Picture two office employees sitting at desks that are less than 3 m apart e-mailing each other about what they are doing for lunch.

Is it possible that over the last 50 to 70 years radio, TV, cinema, video, DVDs, CDs, Walkman, MP3, smart phones, laptops, tablets, computers, and computer games have created a situation where we are in receive mode listening and looking, but not in send mode?

Could the muscles in your voice box, face, and eyes become atrophied or dormant, or be just losing tone and therefore affecting our subtle eye movements, body language, and voice pitch, tone, and volumes that we used to use?

Matthew Hutson, author of the excellent book *7 Laws of Magical Thinking*, talks about this ability and others have also stated that ancient man could detect danger from miles away as can animals on the Serengeti (see also the excellent book *Strategies of the Serengeti* by Stephen Berry). As time has gone on, the need to sense an animal attack from several hundred yards so that we can take evasive action has nearly gone completely and so if we don't use it, we lose it! It is reckoned that last year over 100 people were killed and several hundred were injured or had near misses, by walking into the path of a car while wearing headphones and staring at a smart phone! Car crashes caused by people answering the phone or changing a CD or re-tuning the radio have increased too. These stimuli are taking our focus away from human interaction and into ourselves. If we stop exercises, we get fat and lazy physically—so why can't we get fat and lazy mentally too? Is it possible for our eye muscles and facial muscles, voice boxes, and bodily muscles all historically used to communicate face to face with others, if underused, to become less easy for us to spot the signals from others?

I have noticed an increase in people walking in a slumped head-down pose, trudging along, no/low eye contact and if spoken to, grunt back at us, words of three or four syllables in a monotone, low-pitch, and low-volume way and as the recipient of this the catcher of this behavior cannot decipher it, am confused as to how and what they are really thinking.

People need to get back to looking into each other's eyes, looking for the minute subtle eye flickering movements, where they are really focused. Watching for the muscles in the face creating a slight smile, or frown or surprised look, looking for the tell-tale signs of body language, away from me, toward me, face on, side on, slumped over, standing erect, using or not their hands with appropriate gestures. Are they angry, happy, turned on, excited, stern? How should I reply? It's all part of smart communication, and part of the way of being in which your announcements will somehow need to gain traction to be received and understood.

We are taught as children to treat others how WE want to be treated, but this is wrong and 180 degrees from reality. What people actually want is to be treated how THEY want to be treated. If someone's approach to you is fast and urgent with high levels of energy and speaking quite loudly—then react in the same way. If they are cautious and slower, modest, and shy with a quieter voice—then reciprocate. If they are smiling and happy and joking—then smile back, laugh at their humor, and engage with them for a social chat. If they ask for help and support, then do that. It is called mirroring or matching. It works, and it doesn't affect your personality or your values; it's just that your behavior has changed.

Surely, we need to be trained as children about behavior, a definition, what it actually is, how to read others and themselves, work in teams, groups, and alone. Be responsive to others and learn to read the subtle muscular movements of the face, eyes, and body as well as tuning into the voice pitch, tone, and volume as well as the content to really be able to be effective at communication face to face, online, video conferencing, and even in the written word via e-mail, text, and letters.

Look at this to prove my point, emphasize a different word each time you say this and see how the meaning is dramatically changed and leads to confusion:

> <u>I</u> never said Tim broke your racket.
> I <u>never</u> said Tim broke your racket.
> I never <u>said</u> Tim broke your racket.
> I never said <u>Tim</u> broke your racket.
> I never said Tim <u>broke</u> your racket.
> I never said Tim broke <u>your</u> racket.
> I never said Tim broke your <u>racket</u>.

Thanks to the specific nuances of the English language simply reading the words alone is not enough. The sentence used in that example has just seven words and has seven potential meanings. We need context and we need feeling. That is why one of the fastest growing languages in the world at the moment is the emoji. The happy smiley face and the curly poo are here to stay, and will be joined by others that haven't been invented yet.

Clarifying your message

Whatever form of communication you choose, you will need to formulate a way of ensuring that your content sends the right message in the right way and can be understood by the other person or people involved. In pre-prepared communication, there is an approach that you can use to help you. We call it the content spiral.

The Content Spiral

In order to make your announcements effective, you need to be asking yourself some questions about what you are presenting:

> *Who is the audience?*
> *What do they already know?*
> *What do they need to know?*
> *What do I want them to do?*
> *How much time have I got?*
> *What presentation options do I have?*

If you can answer all these questions, then you can select the content of your announcement and deliver it appropriately.

Let's look at this at the absurd level to prove the point. Let's suppose I'm sitting in a doctors' waiting room and I see somebody running up to throw a bomb in through the window.

What do I do? Let's follow the model:

> *Who is the audience?* Everyone in the room, in fact as many people as I can get to see.
> *What do they already know?* Nothing, I'm the only one who can see this threat.
> *What do they need to know?* That there is a bomb about to come in through the window.

What do I want them to do? Get on the floor to get out of the blast zone.

How much time have I got? Almost none.

What presentation options do I have? Well, I'm introverted, but flashing my eyebrows won't work. If I leap on the ground on my own, they will think I'm mad. I'll have to use my voice.

So what do I do? I yell "Bomb! Get Down" and to support my communication (and to save myself), I throw myself on the floor too. Luckily my actions saved everyone.

It's a simple example, but it actually proves the model really quite well.

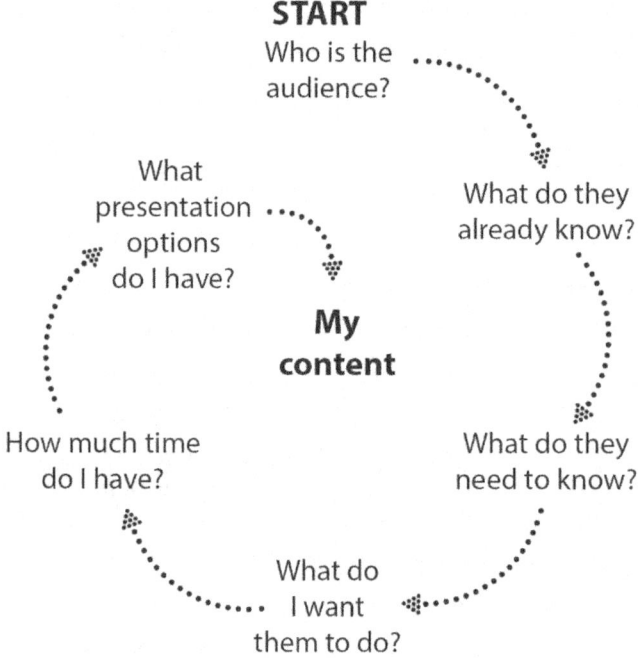

Let's look at another example. I'm about to launch my new brand of shampoo, called Woosh. I'm launching it at a trade show in Berlin, with an audience of 500 people live in the conference hall plus online and broadcast via Facebook live to almost 3,000 people across the globe who might watch it live and another estimated 350,000 who will watch it online but recorded over the next few weeks.

What do I do this time? I follow the same process:

Who's the audience? A real mix of people really, some for retail and some industry commentators and wholesale agents, but potentially they are all customers.

What do they already know? They already know what shampoo is and they might already know about our company through our other products. Our brand has good market penetration in Europe at least.

What do they need to know? That Swoosh is out there and is different and that it is unique with novel chemical agents that give your hair a natural luster and swoosh!

What do I want them to do? Buy Swoosh.

How much time have I got? About 3 minutes.

What presentation options do I have? Loads. Maybe a video, or just a professional piece at the rostrum would be good to make filing easy. I suppose we could support it with great marketing shots of the product and maybe some dancers.

So this one is a bit more tricky, but the process is starting you on a decision-making route that will give you some options to choose from. And while the first example allows for no consultation, the second one does. In this example, a consultation with another person (like a marketing guru, for instance) would help to identify the best option. Don't work alone on communications when you don't have to, your lens is always different to another person.

Making Great Presentations

As a leader or manager, there are many occasions when you will be asked to stand on your feet and deliver a presentation. It might be a project launch, it might be to outline a new process, or it might be to say a few words on the retirement of a colleague. As humans, many of us find these presentations stressful, with the level of discomfort being linked to the number of people in the audience. The more there are, the more nerve wracking it can be. The deeper your degree of introversion, the more uncomfortable this is likely to feel, but introverts can still deliver great presentations. They just need to focus on a few key areas. These are all to do with your body, your behavior, your words, and the feeling that you create in others.

Build connection	Use pace	Persuade
Engage the audience	Present clear data	Use humour!
Show curiosity	Show conviction	Involve a clear call to action
Show understanding	Share a vision	Inspire me

Think about the best presentations that you have seen. Think of the best speeches. What do you remember about them? What would you say about the people who presented them?

Oprah Winfrey delivered a captivating address at the Golden Globes Awards ceremony in January 2018. Her presentation was set against the background of a growing backlash against morally reprehensible behavior and the growing support for the #TimesUp and #MeToo campaigns. In just under 9 minutes, she spoke 1,000 words and delivered one of the most powerful speeches you will ever see.

Why was Oprah's speech so powerful? For a start, it was delivered against a context—it was relevant, topical, and in the moment. But during the speech Oprah captivated her audience, she shared a vision, told stories, showed gratitude and humility, used pace, timing, and the pitch tone and volume of her voice to build emotional content that showed conviction, passion, and a determination for change. She drew on emotion. She showed leadership and made a plea. Most crucially, she included and repeated a very clear "Call to Action," leaving it very clear what she expected the audience to do; "speaking your truth is the most powerful tool we all have."

It was a great presentation and a shining example of the energy that such presentations can bring.

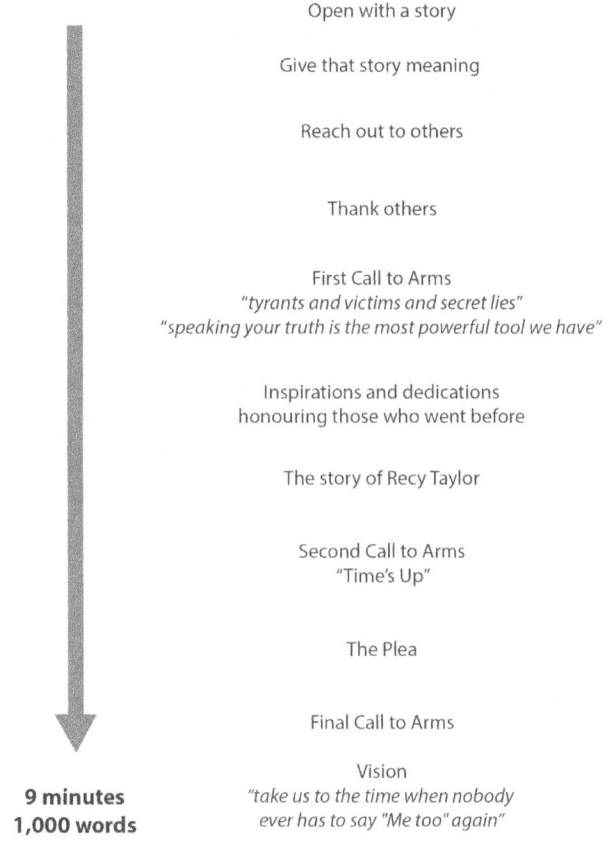

Open with a story

Give that story meaning

Reach out to others

Thank others

First Call to Arms
"tyrants and victims and secret lies"
"speaking your truth is the most powerful tool we have"

Inspirations and dedications
honouring those who went before

The story of Recy Taylor

Second Call to Arms
"Time's Up"

The Plea

Final Call to Arms

Vision
9 minutes   *"take us to the time when nobody*
1,000 words   *ever has to say "Me too" again"*

Analysis of engagement Oprah Winfrey's speech at The Golden Globe Awards, 2018

Delivering Your Message as a Presenter

Body language, and especially your face and eyes, matter significantly for great presentations. Soft eyes flash "friend" messages. Wide eyes signal "fear", like a rabbit caught in the headlights of an oncoming car. Making eye contact also matters, giving your presentation a direct and authentic appeal; and the extroverts who are energized by eye contact will need to see this from you. Move your gaze across the audience and share a moment of eye contact as you go. As you do this, with your soft eyes you will flash friend messages to people, and receive the same back. These friends in the audience can be a great help to ease nerves, so you can flit your eyes to them more than others—but just not all the time, you must remember the other people.

Smile a natural smile. It takes practice but it can be done. Natural smiles involve the eyes. If you can look happy, then you have a better chance of sounding happy and if you can sound happy, then you have a better chance of engaging others.

Your voice should be loud and clear. One of the worst characteristics that you can have as a public speaker is to mumble. The very act of mumbling hunches your shoulders and lowers your chin. These are all bad habits and will not engage your audience. You need to be clear and precise in your words and speak so that others can hear you. Imagine there is a volume dial in the middle of your back, just below and between the shoulder blades. Turning this dial not only raises your voice so that others can hear you but you will speak more clearly, forming your words with more care so that others will hear. This act will also force you to raise your chin, pump out your chest, straighten your back, and improve your breathing.

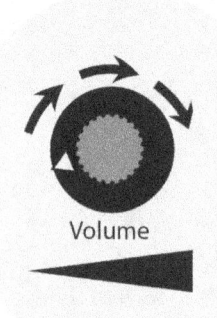

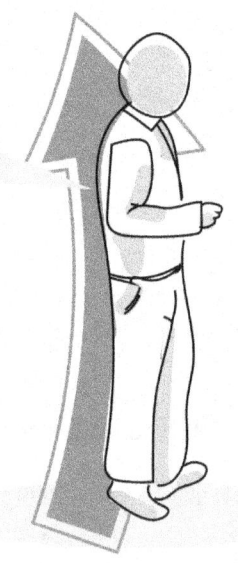

As you turn the imaginary volume control on your back not only does the sound of your voice change, but your chin will come up, you will speak more clearly, your back will straighten, you will breathe more deeply and your whole posture will improve.

Speak up and stand tall

If you follow the volume control technique, then you're already on your way to a good posture. The other thing to remember is your general stance and in the way that you use your hands. Leaning on a table with you knuckles is the presentation style of a silverback gorilla, not an empathetic leader. Sure, you can edge your body forward to show desire, commitment, emphasis, energy, and passion, but use these within a less aggressive pose most of the time. We say to people that it is best to stand comfortably, without crossing your legs, with your feet roughly a shoulder's width apart. Any more than that and you look like you're a gunfighter waiting to pull his six shooter. If you want to see this done badly, just watch any number of normally lily-livered politicians who are told to stand on stage and "be confident." They look like the great Lord Flash-heart character from the Blackadder series (and if you don't know who that is, Google it, you're in for a treat). Your hands should generally not be in your pockets (this can be viewed as informal, but also can be seen as dishonest—it's your call), but instead should be open and not placed across your body. Crossing arms across your body is a natural defence mechanism that goes back all those years to when the first apes went from walking on all fours to walking on two legs. When you walk on all fours, your soft underbelly is protected by the ground. Once you stand up, it becomes very exposed—it's only natural to want to cover that when in times of stress.

Finally, be you. Think about what it is that you want to do as a speaker. What do you want others to think or do differently? Stay focused on that and you will be hitting the right note.

Sure, you can change your posture and the way you speak, but they are all just behavioral changes which in the short term do not change who you are inside. Any announcement or presentation that you make must be seen to come from you. If it's not natural, the audience will not get the emotional content of what you said and the impact of your announcement will be reduced.

How to Support Your Talk?

When people in business talk about their presentation, they normally talk about it as meaning the materials they use to support their talk. Most normally, these are done formulaically using Microsoft PowerPoint, Apple's KeyNote, or Prezi. These are commonly branded, sometimes using a template that was created by a smart cookie in marketing. Some organizations police the use of these slides with gusto, claiming it to be part of their brand experience. Seeing as the B in "Blood, Sweat, and Tears," talks about branding and the importance of the image that it creates it would be a little unfair of us to say this is wrong. But there are times when it should be challenged. Personal messages designed to move or shift the brand must be delivered outside of the restrictions provided by the existing brand. But provided you are allowed some flexibility, you will surely spend some time developing slides that will support your talk. For this, we offer three simple tips:

1. Keep it short
2. Use pictures
3. Avoid bullets

Keep It Short

Presentation software is so easy to use and is such fun to use that it is all too easy to add too many slides. The chances are you will speak for too long and will be boring. If I asked a business person to make me a presentation that spoke about poor moral and social bullying in Hollywood, they would probably deliver a half-hour presentation with 50 slides. Oprah knocked me dead in less than 10 minutes with no slides. Keep it short. Create your presentation and run it through. Then reduce it by half. When you've done that, reduce it by half again. Only when it becomes impossible to repeat this halving are you finally getting to the right length. Nobody wants to suffer death by PowerPoint.

Use Pictures

Wherever you can, use pictures not words. There are a few simple reasons for this. Firstly, you can say with one well-chosen image what you can never say in a slide full of words. Pictures stimulate the emotional side of the audience's brains and allow them to connect with you. The other downside with words is that people read them. And when they are reading the words, they are not listening to you. In a bad presentation, this may be no bad thing as you might even be making the situation a whole lot worse by reading words to me from the slide. PLEASE do not do this.

We train and coach a lot of people to deliver great presentations, and if there is one symptom of a sub-standard presentation that we see a lot in people as they come into our sessions, it is this. Reading the slide drains energy from you and from the audience. On top of that, it normally means that you will be facing the screen or wall when you do it, which by default means that you will not be facing your audience. Stop it.

Avoid Bullets (Where You Can)

There are many people who believe that you cannot use bullet points in presentation. We say that rather depends on the presentation you are giving. You wouldn't expect Tony Robbins to stand up and give a passionate presentation about relationships and self-confidence supported by a slide of bullet points. But you might expect someone who is outlining the top three features of a new finance system to include a slide with three bullets on. As a rule, we say don't use bullets. If you are choosing to use a presentation tool in your talk (and these days we tend to think this is obligatory, but remember it is a choice), we say keep the slides as simple as you can and use as many images as possible. Remember that many people will remember the image far more easily than what you said while it was showing. This goes back to the barking dog from Chapter 2 of our "Blood" book—images speak louder than words. Images capture emotion and stimulate different parts of the brain in a way that bullets do not. Pictures can excite and stimulate an audience. Bullets do not. Maybe instead of using bullets you can use an image to support each point? This makes for more slides but will make your presentation more engaging. It is your choice. Do not be suckered into the trap of using bullets just because it is expected. If you want to be remembered, do something different.

We learn from others, and our first exposure to presentations comes at school where probably 95 percent of teachers are using slides with more bullets than a 1920s gangster shoot out. Not only are these presentations boring our kids, but they are creating a generation of people who think it's OK to fit 10 bullet points on a slide. Our children are being shown from an early age that this kind of thing is acceptable, when in fact it is purely the production of an unimaginative mind. If only we could get teachers to use fewer bullets, we might see less of them in the business presentations of the future. I truly hope so.

Remember These Golden Rules for Announcements and Presentations

Communication matters and it is a human thing.

If it can be misunderstood then it will be misunderstood

Use the content spiral

Inspire your audience - think Oprah!

Smile and flash friend messages

Speak up and stand up

Keep it short

Use images not words

Avoid bullets

And be you, because everybody else is already taken!

CHAPTER 4

R Is for Reviews

Do You Take the Time to Review and Learn from the Past?

"By three methods we may learn wisdom: First, by reflection, which is noblest; Second, by imitation, which is easiest; and third, by experience, which is the bitterest."

—Confucius

A review is an assessment of something to see how good it is and with the intention of instituting change to improve if necessary. It may or may not be formal. A review takes the form of stepping off the hamster wheel of the daily grind to look more carefully at not only what has been done (i.e., rearward assessments of targets and goals), but also looking at how it has been done, and what needs to be different in the future. They are also a great "pause" in the working calendar that allows the purpose of the activity—the "why"—to be refreshed and reinvigorated. Our opinion of reviews at all levels is that they are a must!

In this chapter, we are interested in the following reviews:

A) Reviews of the business
B) Reviews of individuals
C) Reviews of projects
D) Reviews of ourselves

Reviews have certain characteristics. They are focused on acts and things to do or to be done. They delve into the past but their intention is to change the future. They should be multidirectional (i.e., we should review from as many different angles and viewpoints as we can) to remove the impact of bias, groupthink, and our own lens on the world. They should be supportive, not accusatory and they should be completed as part of a process.

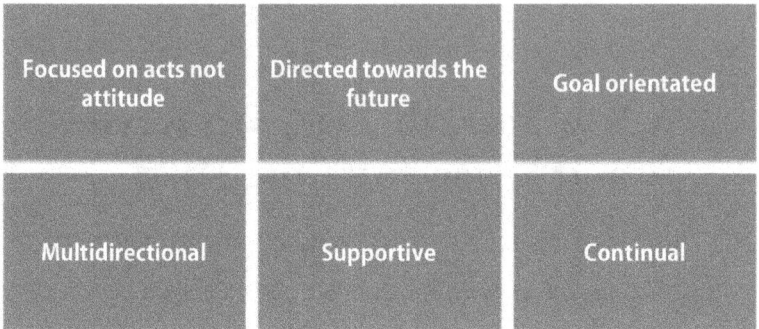

| Focused on acts not attitude | Directed towards the future | Goal orientated |
| Multidirectional | Supportive | Continual |

The best reviews are

Reviews of the Business

We believe that you should regularly take your key performance indicators (KPI) and measure how you are doing—reporting it to the other key senior people in your business and adjusting the plan as required.

KPIs that people usually measure are:

KPI	Poor	Requires improvement	Good	Very good	Excellent
Turnover in a rolling quarter/year					
Sales this week/ today/this month					
Gross profit					
Net profit					
Cost of sales					
Net promoter score (customer feedback)					
Staff survey scores					
Time to fill a vacancy					
Cost of employing a person					
ROI training					
Training spend					

KPI	Poor	Requires improvement	Good	Very good	Excellent
Training days delivered average per employee per year					
Time to deliver product or service after order received					
Sickness and absence					
360-degree feedback scores on managers from staff					
Many others!!					

At your monthly senior team meetings/operations meetings or board meetings, measure these, publish these, and focus on the lower scores as this becomes actions for your direct report.

These can be written as SMART Goals and will be reviewed in 1,2,3,4 weeks' time or at some other sensible interval. They in turn will sub-divide these to their direct reports as smart goals too. Thus, creating a team approach to everyone focused on trying to achieve the same goals and in the same time frames. All pulling together and creating a culture of continuous performance improvement.

But before you hand these out, we need to look at what success is and that the KPIs are stretching, achievable, realistic, and fair to all.

Reviews of Individuals

Aligning the performance of individuals to the goals and aims of the team and the wider business will help create a success. There are many benefits of this process. Reviewing the performance of individuals allows individuals to have important one-to-one time with their manager that is focused entirely on them and how they do their work. It is a great opportunity to have conversations around past performance and future goals, desires, and career ambitions. For managers, they provide the opportunity to redirect employees toward latest business needs, goals, and visions and to formally handle underperformance. A key role of the manager is the performance review. In many business these are normally completed annually (which, incidentally is not frequent enough, they should be reviewed half yearly with monthly and quarterly "mini" reviews), either to a set cycle or on the anniversary of the employee joining the business. They are normally accompanied by an appraisal form that is completed to provide evidence and a basis for discussion, and sit at the heart of the process for setting and reviewing SMART goals (see diagram). Most organizations are poor at this. Forms become a burden and don't really relate to the changing content and demands of peoples' jobs and managers and staff are not trained or supported at having the conversation that is needed to make a change.

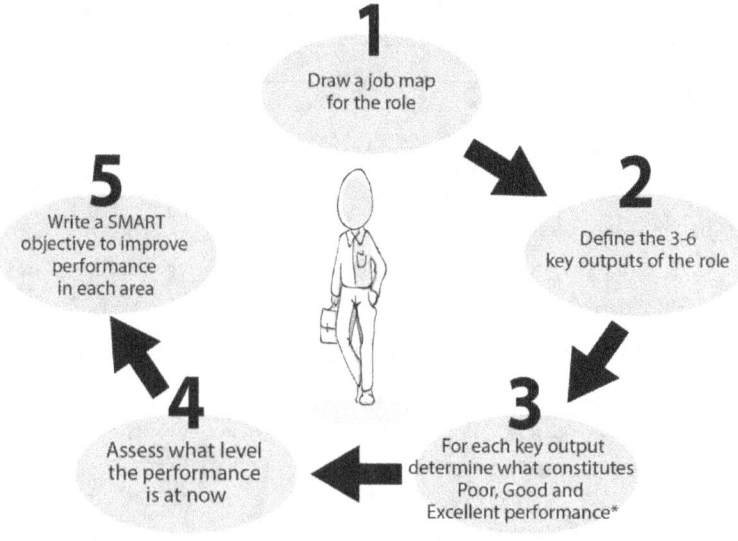

You can also use Poor, Requires Improvement, Average, Above Average, Good and Exceptional

5 steps to SMART objectives (and a basic performance management process)

Conducting Appraisals

If you are conducting these sessions, your job is to ensure a quality conversation with meaningful outputs. The reviews should be conducted in a private space where you will not be disturbed and the other person must have been given reasonable notice of attendance and given the opportunity to ask what they would like to discuss. At the meeting itself, you should make the person feel welcome and explain the purpose of the meeting and the process you will follow as part of the review.

You should also ask the other person if they have any questions about that.

Then, before jumping in with what you think of what they have done, ask them to reflect on their own performance. This should drive a discussion during which it is OK for you to share your opinion and should include the sharing of feedback (more on this below). If your system gives them a "score" as part of the review, this should be shared, along with any information of bonuses or other performance-related aspects of the process. Be prepared for the other person to have a different view. As manager, your role is to guide a discussion on the similarities and differences in the appraisal and explore these and support with detailed feedback—including feedback from others if you can seek and offer it.

Then you can set and agree to expectations for the next period, revisit their job map and key outputs, and agree to the SMART goals. As part of this, you should discuss development opportunities and training needs and schedule your next 121 meeting, which should not be too far into the future (especially if the new goals are at all contentious, unclear of particularly stretching). Then close the meeting and ensure that all paperwork and follow-ups take place.

Reviews are about feedback and form a key part of encouraging others. Giving high-quality feedback to your colleagues is a powerful skill to master; we can use it to redirect and to reinforce. Use this template as part of your preparation to guide you.

What is the behavior, act, performance, or issue that I want to redirect or reinforce?
What detailed examples do I have of the act and its effects?
How recent was the incident? Have I put this off for too long? How truthful is my recollection of it?
Can I identify and describe the results I hope my feedback will produce? What do I really expect to be different as a result of giving this feedback?
Does the other person understand my expectations of performance?
Are the expectations on this person fair and reasonable?
Is the person really responsible for the act/issue/problem in question? (Are you sure it's not you?)
Is the other person open to my feedback? How might I need to deliver it?
What else might be happening for the other person that is affecting their performance?
In what other ways might I and others help them?
How am I going to structure the conversation? Use BEER and PEG.

The BEER Model

It sounds like every drinker's dream. A model of feedback that involves beer. Only it's not the beer that you'd enjoy after work, but is rather a framework that you can use to deliver feedback as part of a review meeting. You can use beer when you wish you identify a piece of poor, substandard, or undesirable behavior by the person that you'd like to change, improve, or correct. It goes a bit like this.

> Stage 1: Behavior—describe the behavior. What did they say or do?
> Stage 2: Effect—what effect did this behavior have on the situation or the people involved?
> Stage 3: Expectation—state what is the expected behavior.
> Stage 4: Result—what do you expect to happen?

Here's an example:

> Not challenging the poor performance of the subcontractor [B] directly led to the project being six weeks late [E]. It's vitally important to challenge any poor performance as soon as it is identified [E] so we can keep the project on target and within budget [R].

Or

> Raising your voice at team members [B] creates an atmosphere in the office which others find demotivating and contributes to a bad atmosphere [E]. People have a right to be treated the way that they want to be treated[E] so we can get the issue resolved in a way that retains a good atmosphere in the team and makes you appear more reasoned [R].

The PEG Model

The PEG model is slightly different in that it looks at Performance—Expectation—Gap.

> Stage 1: Performance: What is happening?
> Stage 2: Expectation: What do you expect to be happening?

Stage 3: Gap: What needs to happen to bridge the gap? (this could be a statement or question)

Like this:

I heard you being very aggressive in the open plan office toward Sally last week [P]. It's important to me that all our people are treated the way that they want to be treated and not treated in that way [E]. Next time that happens, please speak with her in private about the issue [G].

Or maybe

Our contractors are not delivering to timetable on this project [P]. The expectation is that we manage them to ensure they deliver to time [E]. What can you do to get them back on schedule? [G].

Whichever model you use, the main thing in these reviews is to use good questions and listen actively to your responses.

The Impact of SPECTRUM on Performance Reviews

Our behavioral preferences impact the way in which we complete reviews.

When leading a review, the RED manager is direct and challenging, practical, decisive, to the point, and task orientated. He or she will probe and press for outcomes and commitment. In doing this, they may dominate and tell people what to do, opting for action over thought, and create pressure. They can be too assertive and pushy in their attempts to force participants into action and make participants feel uncomfortable.

The GREEN manager is supportive, patient, predictable, easy-going, and calm. He or she will listen actively and allow the emphasis to be on others. They are responsive and eager to collaborate to create best outcomes that can be shared and which they can feel part of. On the negative side, they will also tend to avoid confrontation and be slow to change. They can appear indecisive and can be manipulated and become disillusioned. And when push comes to shove, they would often rather say YES to others who are pushy when they should say NO.

The BLUE manager is accurate and well prepared with an emphasis on good paperwork which they sometimes use as a shield against the human process. They are diplomatic and offer analytical and fact-based feedback which they can support with evidence. In the review, they are cautious, restrained, and methodical and their analysis or thoughts on the future are stable and consistent with no surprises. They can get bogged down in too much detail and their style can be slow and monotone and unaware of the needs of the other person. Their views are strong, needing lots of evidence and time to accept changes so they can be inflexible and appear too cautious and restrained. Their thinking process is deep and they can sometimes fall silent for long periods while the process is happening. They are fine with this although others can see it as being withdrawn.

The YELLOW manager is charming, smiley, and engaging—to your face at least. He or she is sensitive, friendly, enthusiastic, passionate, approachable, and open. They like to involve others and have creative and innovative views of the future where they can see a clear view of the big picture. On the downside, they can be unprepared and disorganized, with not enough detailed information to support their "always" and "never" statements. They can sound insincere and may overexaggerate. Their poor attention to process means they take few notes and can fail to follow-up on agreed actions.

Reviews of Projects

The end of a project is not the end of the project. When a project ends, you may have completed the work or attained the target but the learning from the project is still ongoing. We believe it is vitally important to conduct postproject reviews including all the stakeholders that you used in the project launch or in the premortem that you may have completed at the start. This postmortem can include a reassessment of the premortem. Did the issues and challenges that your thought would materialize actually occur? What other risks arose that threaten or impact delivery? Could you have done something about them? How does that inform your thinking on last time? The size of the project is irrelevant here, although the process that you follow might be slightly different. For instance, if you are an accountant, you might hold a personal project review of how you just completed the latest set of quarterly accounts. If you are a manager, you might conduct a personal review of the appraisal interview you just held with a difficult employee. The key aim of these reviews is to ask yourself "what have I learnt?" And then apply your learning.

For larger projects, we again think this should be a group review that is externally facilitated or led. It should bring as many stakeholders together as possible to ask them the following questions:

Did we achieve our objective?
What went well?
What did not go so well?
What would we want to be different next time around?
What can we do to make that happen?

These sessions must not be rubber-stamp formalities where nothing is challenged. Indeed, the opposite is true. They should be honest and with some deep challenges of process, actions, and beliefs. The outcomes should be captured and disseminated and any actions must be owned by somebody who is empowered to take them forward. This review action and review are part of learning. The sad truth is that many businesses either do not perform reviews or simply pay them lip service and then do not act on the outcomes. Teams are broken up, mistakes and over-runs are brushed under the carpet, individuals are scapegoated for their role in the project, and the mistakes are repeated next time around. The best project leaders and managers should be tackling this and prioritizing these reviews and recognizing them as the best opportunity they have to actually learn from doing something. They generate the evidence that you need to be the catalyst for change.

Reviews of Ourselves

The art of self-reflection and development ties into many other areas of this book. To be at your best, you need to be open to and respectful of feedback from others, which you should crave. Think of the last time that someone offered you some negative or developmental feedback. What did you do?

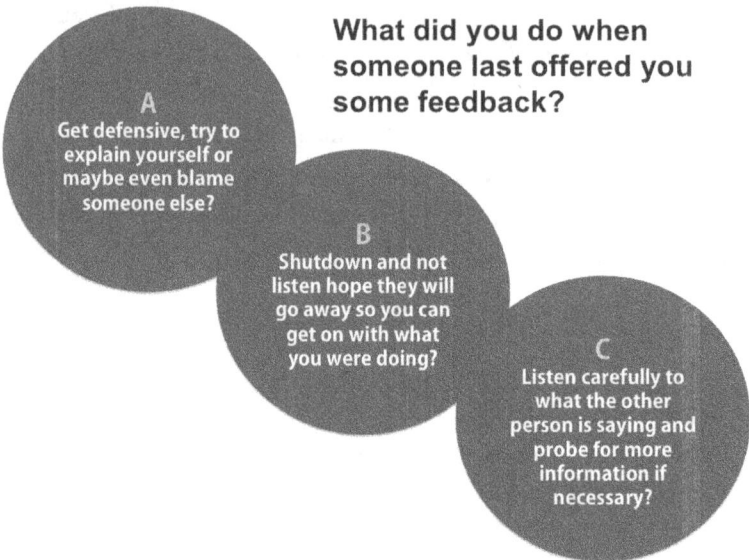

What did you do when someone last offered you some feedback?

A
Get defensive, try to explain yourself or maybe even blame someone else?

B
Shutdown and not listen hope they will go away so you can get on with what you were doing?

C
Listen carefully to what the other person is saying and probe for more information if necessary?

Did you get defensive, try to explain yourself, or even maybe try to blame someone else? Did you shutdown, discredit them, and hope that they will go away so that you can get on with what you were doing? Did you listen carefully to what they were saying and probe for more information? Did you do something else? Did you act on their feedback?

In truth, many of us are poor at taking onboard feedback, accepting it only when it comes from people to whom we attribute power or if we see it for ourselves. Developing a growth mindset, which you are showing by reading and acting on the content of this book, will allow you to develop the skills to get better at this. Listen to what people have to say to you. As we mentioned under the ENCOURAGEMENT chapter, surround yourself with people who can give you that feedback and who want to help shape you into the best person you can be.

Reflecting helps you to develop your skills and review their effectiveness, rather than just carry on doing things as you have always done them. A study of customer service representatives found that those who regularly reflected on their training performed 25 percent better on the final test than other trainees. They also improved their chance of receiving the highest rating for their service by 20 percent.[1] It is about questioning, in a positive way, what you do and why you do it, and then deciding whether there is a better, or more efficient, way of doing it in the future.

Here are some helpful questions to get you started with self-reflection, which we think could be included in your weekly schedule for maximum impact:

Strengths—What are my strengths?

Weaknesses—What are my weaknesses?

Skills—What skills do I have and what am I good at?

Problems—What problems are there at work/home that may affect me?

Achievements—What have I achieved (recently) and how did that feel?

Happiness—Are there things that I am unhappy with or disappointed about? What makes me happy? What needs to happen in the next (week) to keep my happiness levels up?

Solutions—What could I do to improve in these areas?

Having a growth mindset is about increasing your self-efficacy. By reviewing our own performance and reflection on our own behaviors, challenges, and desires, we allow ourselves to explore the territory in which we can feel more confident, capable, focused, and certain of our ability to achieve our goals. This process itself is enough to help us improve. While the resilience this develops might be psychological, it is in fact impossible to separate it from the way you approach the practical or cognitive aspects of your work. By reflecting on past experience and performance, we refine and redefine our knowledge of exactly how we achieved what we did, giving us clearer goals and greater ability, and allowing us to unlock the potential that lurks within us all.

---

[1]Di Stefano, G., F. Gino, G.P. Pisano, and B.R. Staats. 2016. "Making Experience Count: The Role of Reflection in Individual Learning." Working paper, NOM Unit Working Paper No. 14-093, Harvard Business School, Boston.

Remember These Golden Rules about Reviews

If you never know where you are, you'll never know when you've arrived.

Reviews are an important part of the learning process and allow you to improve.

Review timetables are important.

There is nothing that you do that cannot be reviewed.

Reviews must be honest, goal focused, multidirectional, and supportive.

A review that isn't acted upon is wasted.

CHAPTER 5

S Is for Success

Can You Deliver Success for You, Your Team, and Your Business?

"The only place where success comes before work is in the dictionary!"
—Vince Lombardi

Success is the accomplishment of an aim or purpose and the good or bad outcome of an undertaking. Most of us want to be successful. It's what drives our actions—and your own quest for it is probably one of the reasons why you are reading this book.

Success is a movable end game depending on where you start, so for some of us getting out of bed in the morning is success, or maybe not having a cigarette or an alcoholic drink is a success. Losing a pound on a diet or getting through the day could be successful for some people. In business, we usually mean winning, getting to yes, getting past no, hitting your target, meeting a deadline, having happy customers and staff are all measures of success. So, before you start anything, put down on paper what you feel success will look like at the end, when you have achieved it, and then every day, look at it and see if you are still working toward that aim.

We say success is when you aim to achieve something and manage to do it, on time, to budget, to the standard you wanted, and with happy staff and happy customers and that if you went back and started again, would you do it any differently?

The Feeling of Success

Over the years, we have run many workshops for clients. Many of these are focused on creating team engagement and alignment. On these sessions, one of the first exercises that we commonly run is to ask people to think of a moment in their life when they were "at their best" and to summarize that feeling in just one word. The responses are always personal, but there are some words that appear more frequently than others. *Proud, happy, satisfied, confident, motivated,* and *successful* all appear alongside other strong emotions such as *buzzing, unstoppable, awesome, joyful, amazing,* and *euphoric.* It's an enabling and emotional experience that brings color to the cheeks, puffs out the chest, and allows people to walk tall and look the world in the eye. It's a powerful feeling and a moment when people are at their most engaged and energized feel.

When we explore some of the stories behind the words, there is a theme that emerges for most of these are words that are drawn from experiences that happened outside of the workplace. It is typical that of the stories we hear that elicit these feelings, around 90 percent relate to a personal milestone. Few relate to on-the-job experiences. It is perhaps not surprising that people's best moments of success, pride, and happiness are associated with personal experiences, but wouldn't it be wonderful if we could more commonly associate these feelings with our work? When we do this exercise with teams, we talk about the feelings of success that people experience at work and how they are sometimes more elusive and less common, and we explore the reasons why that may be the case. Sadly, in some groups, the experience of success at work is alien, but in the work that follows, we allow them to explore what forms success might take, how they can achieve it, and some of the feelings that accompany that outcome.

Success at the Business or Team Level

Let's drop our minds back to the previous chapter for a moment, where we introduced the review table for business performance. Here, we have this same scorecard containing the same KPIs, but this time with some actual numbers in so that we can see what "good" looks like and know that we have been successful in our quest or not.

KPI	Poor	Requires improve-ment	Good	Very good	Excellent
Turnover in a rolling quarter/year	Worse than 10% below target	£XM–10%	£XM	Up to 5% above target	More than 5% above target
Sales this week/today/ this month	Below 400,000 a week	400,000–499,999 a week	£500,000 a week	£5000,001–£999,999 a week	Over £1M a week
Gross profit	Below 20%	21%–29%	30%	31%–40%	40% +
Net profit	Less than 8%	9%	10%	11%	12%
Cost of sales (everything added together)	Above 250,000 a week	Up to 250,000 a week	100,000 a week	Less than 100,000	Less than 80,000
Net promoter score (customer feedback)	5/10	6/10	7/10	8/10	9/10
Staff survey scores	5	6	7	8	9
Time to fill a vacancy	3 months	2 months	1 month	3 weeks	1 week
Cost of employing a person	150%+	126%–150%	125% of annual salary per employee per year	124%–120%	Less than 120%
ROI training	0%	1%–4%	5% increase in sales	6%–9% increase	9% and above
Training spend You could argue here that actually more spent is a good thing not a bad thing !!!!	7%+	6%	5% turnover	4% turnover	3% turnover

(continued)

(continued)

KPI	Poor	Requires improvement	Good	Very good	Excellent
Training days delivered average per employee per year	Less than 3	4	5 days per year	6–9 days	10+
Time to deliver product or service after order received	1 week	36 hours	24 hours	12 hours	6 hours
Sickness and absence	7%+	6%	5% of all staff away at any one time	4%	3%
360-degree feedback scores on managers from staff	5/10	6/10	7/10	8/10	9/10
Health and safety	5+ reported incidents in a given period	2–5 reported incidents in a given period	2 reported incidents in a given period or whatever you feel is appropriate—near misses, deaths, major injuries, hazards reported, etc.—choose what is right for your business	1 reported incident in a given period	No reported incidents in a given period
Add as many as you want					

We have included here some example values. We recommend that you take this table and recreate it for your business. Of course, your business might already have these metrics, they might exist in a business plan, or in a targets document of stated key indicators that you work against every year, quarter, month, week, or day. Only measure meaningful things for your business—if it isn't important to you or your customers, forget it. What we think is important is the recognition and celebration that should happen when you hit these targets. It is OK to celebrate and reward hard work. In fact it is essential. This does not only mean financial rewards (think back to what we said about motivation in the ENCOURAGEMENT chapter), but will need to be different for each person. As we've already said, nothing motivates like success and if you can keep your business, the teams within it, and the individuals themselves constantly moving toward their development goals, then your hard work will pay dividends. Recruit great people and then get out of their way.

As your business succeeds in hitting these targets, part of your ongoing improvement process will be to review and rethink. As your business hits "excellent" in each of the KPI areas described, you should firstly celebrate the achievement and recognize the efforts of those who got you there, but also think where to go next? Do not rest on your laurels. Look at the table and perform a column shift. As your business grows, what you once thought of as excellent norm becomes the new norm, and new excellent appears on the planning horizon.

This process, while being testing, challenging, and motivational, can also at times feel negative, as if each stage of excellent is not good enough. Make sure you and your people have time to celebrate their victory before you march off toward new goals.

Personal Success

Personal success is, well, more personal. Like the story of Alice in Wonderland meeting the Cheshire Cat, if you don't know where you are going, then any route will take you there. Sometimes we can be our own worse critics, always striving for more. It is OK to be sitting at a beach with a cocktail in your hand and have a fast car parked in your garage at home—enjoy the profits of your hard work.

Never feel guilty about celebrating your success—reward yourself with the things that you like the most to do—if that is charity, fast cars, holidays, quality time with your friends and family, then do it. Personal success comes in all forms, of which professional achievement and mastery is just one. What does personal success mean to you? Only you know, but what we know is that your success in business is built on how well you can apply "Blood, Sweat, and Tears."

CHAPTER 6

Conclusions

"I am slowly coming to the conclusion that it's more important to learn to work with what you've got, under the circumstances you've been given, than wishing for different ones."

—Charlotte Eriksson

Sometimes we learn fast. Swing one punch and you'll make contact, but swing another and I'll duck. That's fast learning. But learning just why it was that you wanted to punch me in the first place takes a little longer. For that to happen, I need to learn about you, and I need to learn about me, and I need to learn what it is about our relationship that stimulates the Frank Bruno tendencies in you. Learning comes via action, and learning from that action through the act of reflection.

Learning isn't always easy. It is often challenging. Ever heard the phrase "I learn most when I'm out of my comfort zone"? Well, it may be true, but life outside the comfort zone (and maybe I'll revisit just what a comfort zone is in another blog entry one day) comes with lots of other challenges that might actually restrict learning.

We are all on a learning journey. Learning starts as soon as a new born baby learns how to breathe in air and stops, arguably, when we learn what it is to be dead. At all points in between, we are weaving our learning journey. This journey can be enriched by learning how to learn, and this starts with a journey of self-discovery.

To misquote another famous saying: "To learn about others, you must first learn about yourself." This has a ring of truth about it. Knowing our own preferences, bias, and strengths helps us to understand who we are, and helps us to understand how others see us. I accept that I am shaped by a lifetime of unique experiences and influences that make me different from you. My learning allows me to be confident in my own power, a sort of self-assurance and personal gravitas that has given me the ability to identify, stimulate, and pursue an inquiry. In our own experiences, it has given us the opportunity, drive, and more importantly the courage, to launch businesses. Most notably though, it has given us the ability to finally know who we are as people, and to be comfortable with that. This is a prize that's been worthy of any investment made.

Now that you have read "Tears" and hopefully have already read "Blood" and "Sweat," what final advice can we offer you as you embark on your continued journeys of self-development?

Firstly, **accept yourself as data**. Your experiences are valid. The thoughts, feelings, and experiences that you have are yours and are real. Don't be dictated to by others (and yes, there is a certain irony in even writing that in a list of tips!). Take as much information as you can from situations. Reflection is a key tool. Assimilate your data, your thoughts, your feelings, your observations, your history, and turn these into learning. You know your strengths and your weaknesses—and seek feedback from others. Notice how your strengths and weaknesses and hopes and fears affect you and drive your choices. When important things happen, take time to notice your own feelings and responses. Notice the emotional responses and the line of thought that they provoke. It's all data. Record these feelings. Junkies of this kind of thing use a reflective diary to capture all that stuff. It's not necessary, but some find it helpful.

Secondly, **do not fear change**, accept it as an opportunity to take action to live a diverse existence. Again, recognize your thoughts and feelings. Take note of the internal dialogue that goes on as you wrestle over decision making and fears of change. You can take learning from that. To develop is to change. It is in the nature of the journey.

Measure twice and cut once—it is always better to be safe than sorry.

Allow time for yourself. All of us, whether we are parents, children, husbands, wives, managers, or coworkers, may sometimes feel blocked by the world around us. To learn is to accept that to be a perfectly normal and shared experience. Following your own learning path sometimes means that you have to be selfish. Don't be afraid to take some "me time" when you need to. Recognize and satisfy your own needs. For many of us, this is not as easy as it sounds. It can be hard to be selfish when others need you. But sometimes you have to be hard. To learn is to develop an appropriate level of assertiveness to enable you to hold a space for what needs to be done. Use the SPECTRUM model to help you. It works.

Love what you do. And if you don't love it, don't do it. Lots of things will catch your eye, but only a few catch your heart. Pursue those, talk about them passionately, and indulge your time on them. At the same time, expect all your employees to love what they do too; it is OK to have fun at work. Even undertakers and funeral directors have fun at work.

If you don't know something, just ask. You can learn a lot about yourself through feedback from others. You'd be surprised how many people will give you honest feedback if you ask the right way. Good questions such as "What did you think of the way I did X?" or "I'd like to get better at Y . . . could you suggest any changes I might make?" are all good ways of drawing out ideas from others. But then you must listen. Listen to the responses that others give to you, and if you don't understand it, or if you feel it's unclear, then simply ask them to clarify. Often, and I think this is especially true in organizations, we build up fantasies about why other people do what they do, or what type of lives they have, or how they think. Sometimes we waste time tip-toeing softly around an issue that might not be real at all. You want to know if they think you're a good Project Manager? Just ask responsible questions. Step into your power. It sounds absurd, but its validity is proven.

Learn to be responsible. Sometimes we all feel that we can't get out of a situation. We might feel that things are being done to us to keep us in a less-than-perfect state. "I can't change that," for instance. Sometimes looking at it from a position of responsibility can help to determine a course of action. You can learn to change it.

Take a whole-system focus. We wrote this book so that a new business could start up, an existing business could review where they and for you as a team leader, manager, or leader to drive their own self-development. It should help you to ensure that you don't overlook the things that many do; ensure that you are making a real profit, that as many of the stakeholders as possible are happy, you are in control, and can easily move the business forward using simply tried and tested methods without confusion or fuss.

It hasn't got everything in it you need, or it would be an encyclopedia, but it does contain our knowledge and wisdom. The knowledge of wisdom of our customers and their failures too; after all, we learn more from our failures and have more of them, than we do successes.

We believe it does just that. Now you can run your business with "Blood, Sweat, and Tears."

Your Learning

That brings us to the end of our trilogy. If you have read all three volumes of this book then you have completed our tour of what we see as the key characteristics and actions that can bring success in business. There are other things of course and there are bound to be areas that we have left out simply due to the constraints of space. But in this book, we have given you 15 significant areas of focus to help you define your own successes.

What happens next is up to you. You might want to start with a review of what meaning this book has had for you and how you might apply some of the ideas, challenges, and suggestions that it contains:

Look back at the areas in this book and ask yourself these questions:

Which three of the areas we have identified and discussed do you feel most confident about in terms of your own work?

Area 1: _____

Area 2: _____

Area 3: _____

What evidence do you have to support this?

_____

_____

_____

How does this affect the way that you work?

_____

_____

_____

_____

_____

Which three areas do you feel least confident about in your own performance or ability?

Area 1: _____

Area 2: _____

Area 3: _____

What evidence do you have to support this?

_____

_____

_____

What would you like to be different? (identify three things)

1. _____
_____
_____
_____
_____
_____

2. _____
_____
_____
_____
_____
_____

3. _____
_____
_____
_____
_____
_____

What will you do to start your journey toward these three development goals? And who can help you?

For Goal 1, I will _____

_____

_____

_____

With support from _____

_____

_____

_____

For Goal 2, I will _____

_____

_____

_____

With support from _____

_____

_____

_____

For Goal 3, I will _____

_____

_____

_____

With support from _____

_____

_____

_____

And finally . . .

When will you review your progress against each of these?

Goal 1_____

Goal 2_____

Goal 3_____

There you have it. As we said at the very beginning of this book, much of this is not rocket science but is the application of targeted best practice. We hope that you have enjoyed reading the contents of these pages and that you have found within them some simple practices and concepts that can help you achieve your own goals and dreams and drive yourself, and your business, to success. You've set yourself some goals to keep you moving toward your goal. This will take commitment and a growth mindset and a resilience that will set you apart from the rest. It will also take *Blood, Sweat, and Tears*.

Good Luck!

Index

OTHER TITLES IN THE ENTREPRENEURSHIP AND SMALL BUSINESS MANAGEMENT COLLECTION

Scott Shane, Case Western University, *Editor*

- *African American Entrepreneurs: Successes and Struggles of Entrepreneurs of Color in America* by Michelle Ingram Spain and J. Mark Munoz
- *How to Get Inside Someone's Mind and Stay There: The Small Business Owner's Guide to Content Marketing and Effective Message Creation* by Jacky Fitt
- *Profit: Plan for It, Get It—The Entrepreneurs Handbook* by H.R. Hutter
- *Navigating Entrepreneurship: 11 Proven Keys to Success* by Larry Jacobson
- *Global Women in the Start-up World: Conversations in Silicon Valley* by Marta Zucker
- *Understanding the Family Business: Exploring the Differences Between Family and Nonfamily Businesses, Second Edition* by Keanon J. Alderson
- *Growth-Oriented Entrepreneurship* by Alan S. Gutterman
- *Founders* by Alan S. Gutterman
- *Entrepreneurship* by Alan S. Gutterman
- *Sustainable Entrepreneurship* by Alan S. Gutterman
- *Startup Strategy Humor: Democratizing Startup Strategy* by Rajesh K. Pillania
- *Can You Run Your Business With Blood, Sweat, and Tears? Volume I: Blood* by Stephen Elkins-Jarrett and Nick Skinner
- *Can You Run Your Business With Blood, Sweat, and Tears? Volume II: Sweat* by Stephen Elkins-Jarrett and Nick Skinner

Announcing the Business Expert Press Digital Library

Concise e-books business students need for classroom and research

This book can also be purchased in an e-book collection by your library as

- a one-time purchase,
- that is owned forever,
- allows for simultaneous readers,
- has no restrictions on printing, and
- can be downloaded as PDFs from within the library community.

Our digital library collections are a great solution to beat the rising cost of textbooks. E-books can be loaded into their course management systems or onto students' e-book readers.

The **Business Expert Press** digital libraries are very affordable, with no obligation to buy in future years. For more information, please visit **www.businessexpertpress.com/librarians**. To set up a trial in the United States, please email **sales@businessexpertpress.com**.

www.ingramcontent.com/pod-product-compliance
Lightning Source LLC
Chambersburg PA
CBHW071216220526
45468CB00002B/630